Psychological
Fitness

by *Richard Corriere, Ph.D.*
and *Joseph Hart, Ph.D.*

21 Days to

HBJ

PSYCHOLOGICAL FITNESS

Feeling Good

Harcourt Brace Jovanovich

New York and London

Printed in the United States of America

Library of Congress Cataloging in Publication Data

Corriere, Richard.
   Psychological fitness.

Bibliography: P.
Includes index.
1. Success. 2. Mental health.
I. Hart, Joseph Truman, 1937–   Joint author.
II. Title.
BF637.S8C66   158'.1   78-14073
ISBN 0-15-175280-x

First edition

B   C   D   E

Richard Corriere

I dedicate this book to a number of people in my life. First, to Sam Mitnick, who has guided us and believed in our work since the beginning. Second, to all my friends, who make my own fitness possible. And then, to all the people who have tried as we have to change the direction of their lives because of what they feel. To Peggy Brooks, our editor, who took a beast with many heads and tamed it. And Linda Cirincione, who lets people know about what we do. And Nina Lasagna, who helps me run my life. And finally to my wife, my daughter, and my dog—who give me the love that makes my life come alive.

Joseph Hart

I dedicate this book to my mother and father.

PART 3

How to Change Problems into Strengths

CONTENTS

Foreword

This is a different kind of self-help book. It does not emphasize relaxation or fair fighting or positive thinking or being your own best friend or knowing the games people play. Those are all good and useful activities, but they fall short of what people most need to do for themselves.

Most self-help books are limited to one psychological weakness and how to change it or one type of strength and how to develop it (shyness/assertiveness, nervousness/positive thinking). They do not teach an integrated program or philosophy of self-development that can be used in all aspects of a person's life. They are further limited in that they pay too much attention to correcting weaknesses rather than conveying a real sense and understanding of what it is like to live from psychological strengths.

In the psychological fitness approach you begin by using strengths you already have but do not fully use. From a position of strength you can then go on to change personality weaknesses into new strengths.

Psychological fitness is concerned with getting in shape, building up, and achieving peak psychological performances in your life. The question of course is "how?" If you came to our fitness training programs we could show you in a personal and step-by-step way what to do and how to do it. But most people can't. This book (and the advice it gives) is the next best thing to letting us show you in person.

More than fifteen years have passed since President John F. Kennedy dramatically brought physical fitness into the awareness of the American public. Today more and more people are stretching and running and playing to keep fit.

What we now need is an awareness of the necessity, the possibility, and the methods of psychological fitness. Most people have not yet learned about the psychological side of fitness. People usually believe that taking action psychologically is only for people with psychological problems. But the time for action is before problems arise. Psychological fitness can benefit anyone.

Psychological fitness is a way of getting the most from your personality. It gives you more resistance to stress, and you feel better. When people are psychologically out of balance they need to exercise their weaker areas. The personality, just like the body, must strengthen all its parts to attain fitness.

The first principle of psychological fitness is:

PRINCIPLE ONE: The personality needs to be exercised. Without exercise the personality becomes rigid and deteriorates; it loses its natural elasticity and vitality.

We call the beginning exercises of psychological fitness mind-jogging exercises because they are easy. Mind jogging is just like physical jogging. You do it at a pace that is comfortable for you. The more that you do it, the more fit you become. The first stages of mind jogging are just to get you into shape. The regular practice of mind jogging for just three weeks will help you cope with a wide range of problems and stresses. In this book we are going to help you understand how to become psychologically fit and give you the exercises you need to begin your fitness training.

PART I

The Keys to Psychological Fitness

Strengths, Weaknesses, and the Fitness Philosophy

Psychology and psychiatry have in the past overfocused on illness and disease. It is difficult to feel good about yourself while you are focusing on what is wrong. From the psychological fitness perspective the basic question to be asked is: "What is right with me?" The answers, as we shall see, reveal your strengths.

WHAT IS STRENGTH?

The second principle of psychological fitness says:

PRINCIPLE TWO: Everyone has definite psychological strengths, even the most severely ill or psychologically disturbed. But most people don't have all the skills they need to use their strengths fully.

Joan was a chronic worrier. When we asked her what strengths she possessed she said, "I'm a good housekeeper; I'm a good cook; I'm a good lover; I'm a good mother; I'm a good wife—but I worry about all of those, so *none* of those are strengths." What Joan didn't know was that her greatest strength was hidden in her worrying.

If Joan could have measured all the energy she was using worrying, she would have seen that she was a powerhouse. Instead she told herself that worrying was bad. She needed the energy that went into worrying in other areas of her life. Through fitness training Joan acquired the skills to transfer her negative worrying into positive caring. She learned to stop using her psychological strengths against herself.

It will take time and different chapters of this book to help you discover what *hidden* strengths you have. For now, try this mini-exercise:

A MINI-EXERCISE
THINK ABOUT SOME OF YOUR PERSONAL STRENGTHS. Period. Don't do anything else. It is the same as stretching your legs before you go running. Enjoy focusing on what you do well.

What matters most in *beginning* to develop and learn about your psychological strengths is your perspective. Instead of thinking about what is wrong with you, your weaknesses, we want you to look for your strengths and begin improving what you already have available to you.

THE FITNESS PERSPECTIVE: FOCUSING ON STRENGTHS

The third basic principle of psychological fitness says:

PRINCIPLE THREE: People have been taught to focus on their weaknesses. This focus in and of itself leads to the develop-

ment of poor self-images, negative thoughts, and psychological problems.

Because many people believe that their personalities are as
set as their height or shoe size, they often think about themselves in a rigid way: "I'm just a depressed person," "I'm
moody," "I always have highs and lows," "I'm naturally
shy," or "I came from an unhappy family."

We want you to change these habits. If you are using your
weaknesses more than your strengths, then you need to develop new skills as the following story shows.

A SUNDAY AFTERNOON

One Sunday afternoon not long ago a group of our
friends was playing basketball at a local high school gym.
One of the men we play with is a dark-haired and energetic psychiatrist. He usually is captain of one of the
teams. He has a special knack for finding just the right
position for each player on a team. He knows how to use
everybody's particular strengths to field a good and
competitive squad.

He organized our team. But something was missing.
The old spark was gone. He put us in correct positions
and told us what to do. But soon after the game started
it was obvious that we were going to have trouble with
the other team. By half time we were losing badly. His
shooting and passing were off and, more importantly,
his lively spirit and encouragement were gone.

During the half we pulled him aside and asked what
was wrong. He told us that he had had another big fight
with his wife. He hadn't slept well last night. He felt depressed and hopeless. He complained he was tired of
patching up their problems.

It was obvious that from all of his professional training
he knew what was wrong with his marriage, with his
wife, and with himself. He was paid to know what was
wrong with everybody and everything.

We didn't have much time before the second half
started. We said, "We'll make a bet with you. We will ask
you three questions. If the answers don't make you feel
better we will buy the beers after the game. But if they

do make you feel better you have to really turn this game around—and buy the beer."

He agreed. Here are the three questions that we asked him:

1. What is right with your marriage?
2. Do you love your wife?
3. Do you want to be happily married?

By the time he had finished answering all three questions he was grinning from ear to ear. We hadn't solved any of the basic things he and his wife needed to work out between them, but we started him thinking differently. As soon as he took the fitness perspective he stopped focusing on what was wrong with his marriage. When he remembered what was satisfying and emotionally meaningful about his marriage it became obvious that he didn't need to be down and out just because he and his wife had fought.

In emergencies or crises people often fall back on their weaknesses. They become more rigid at the time when they need to become more flexible. One of our friend's finest strengths was his ability to love. He loved his wife. She had been a loyal, good friend all through medical school and a lover since the day they first met. When they fought he forgot how much he loved her. That forgetting made him feel weak and hopeless. Just before we went back out to play, he said, "I know I feel better—but why?"

We laughed. "It's obvious you have a tremendous gift for organizing this basketball team. You know how to use everyone's individual strengths for the good of the entire team. But in your own life, you aren't using your strengths to get what you really want. When you and your wife fight you both use your weaknesses. It's no wonder you wind up feeling rotten afterwards. You blame each other, you badger each other, you find fault with each other. You focus on what is *wrong*. We're teaching you how to improve what is *right*. All we did was to get you to focus on your strengths. We got you to admit your strengths. That made you feel strong."

As he remembered what was right with him, his strength

of loving, he got a sense that what he was fighting about wasn't as important as it once seemed. In mobilizing his strengths, we had indirectly taught him the first principles of psychological fitness.

BEGINNING TO FIND YOUR STRENGTHS

Follow this next little exercise and you will find that you already have some strengths that you might not be admitting and using.

   1. What are a few of your strengths?
      List two or three.
   2. Do you want to love yourself?
   3. Do you want to feel good?

Your answers are putting in motion strengths that you already have. Once the strengths are set in motion they will naturally tend to stay in motion unless you stop them.

MIND JOGGING

Focusing on your strengths is actually the first step toward mind jogging. Mind jogging is "taking action" psychologically. There are many different kinds of actions we will teach you to take. Some are general exercises, some are designed for certain problem areas, and others for particular kinds of people.

The more comfortable you become mind jogging, the more powerful you will feel. Psychological fitness turns many problems into opportunities to take action, to become stronger, and to test your ability to respond effectively. You no longer worry about whether you are going to make it through one more day—you move naturally and easily through each day as you mind jog.

Mind jogging brings about an awareness of the inner self. Too often we don't get down to this satisfying part of our personalities. Instead, we interact with the world from our outer self.

The awareness you first get from mind jogging soon shifts from the discovery of your inner self to the realization that often your inner self and outer self are out of synch; your thoughts and feelings don't match your actions. Psychological fitness brings thoughts, feelings, and actions into harmony. Mind jogging then is the process of uniting your inner and outer selves.

When your inner self and outer self are not synchronized, you have problems; you are in conflict with yourself and the world around you. Because you don't feel right, you cannot use your strengths. Instead you spend your energy just trying to hold yourself together.

When you have harmony between your inner self and your outer self, you are no longer fighting an inner war. This bringing together is the most satisfying experience you can have psychologically, one you will seek over and over just for that reason. But it also leads to a different way of dealing with your problems. It is the reason for mind jogging.

INNER SELF AND OUTER SELF

Your inner self consists of all your potentials. It is the sense that you have that tells you you are different. This inner self is good. It keeps you alive and going even when you seem to be overwhelmed by the outside world. No matter what happens to you your inner self goes on. It is your awareness of yourself.

Your outer self is the you in the real world, the you who acts, talks, works, plays, has sex, thinks. Your outer self is you in public.

Jeff looks as if he is in good shape. He's thirty-eight years old, is only five pounds overweight, and works hard. He has a drive to succeed. That drive is a strength. Outwardly he pushes himself unmercifully. He doesn't know what else to do. The harder he works the more the pressure builds. He is becoming a success. The pressure continues to build until one evening, while having a bad nightmare, he has his first major heart attack. No one on the outside could tell, but his inner self and outer self were at war. His inner self knew how tired and tense he was. He sensed that he needed to change his lifestyle. But his outer self wanted to reach more goals. They never met until that night when he almost died.

Judy had what she wanted—a husband, a family, and a career. She worked from six A.M. to eleven P.M. doing everything she needed to keep it all together. No one seemed to notice that she was falling apart—the 5 mg of Valium three times a day and the three to four drinks kept everything calm on the surface. But then, when she got her promotion, her world began crumbling. The extra pressures with the new responsibilities were met with additional doses of Valium, more frequent drinks, and new psychological breakdowns. She began to feel irritable with her husband and children. Her anxiety increased. She began to feel afraid. One night while making love with her husband she began to cry. She couldn't stop. Two days later she was delirious in a private hospital. No one around her knew that her inner self and outer self were locked in battle. She had inner needs that her outer self ignored.

Both Jeff and Judy had conflicts between their inner and outer selves—conflicts which they didn't have the skills to resolve.

A conflict occurs when your outer self and your inner self do not match: when your inner thoughts, feelings, and beliefs and your outer actions are not the same. When a person does not possess the skills he needs to resolve this conflict, he begins using unfit behaviors. The man in the previous example did not have the skills he needed to overcome the distance between his inner need to rest and relax and his outer compulsion to work hard and get ahead. The woman did not have the skills to resolve the conflict between what she did on the outside and how she felt on the inside. Both of these people were having serious breakdowns in their lives. Of course, not everyone has such obvious breakdowns.

Many people know enough to keep themselves from having psychological breakdowns. But very few know how to go further and become psychologically fit.

PSYCHOLOGICAL FITNESS AND
MIND JOGGING

We have defined psychological fitness as the ability of a person to enjoy himself or herself day by day and to respond effectively to emergencies and crises. Mind jogging is the activity or exercise that gets you ready for more pleasure and helps turn crises into problems with solutions.

You are going to change your personal philosophy when you find your inner self—just as you change your perspective on your physical potential when you get into shape. Your inner self gives you an internal reference to guide your behavior, so you no longer follow by rote outer rules and regulations about what is right and what is wrong.

When you are psychologically fit, you live from an inner sense of what feels good and what doesn't. You harmonize your life and no longer resist the basic energy which comes from your inner self. When you bring your inner self and outer self into harmony you have extra energy to use, because you aren't trying to hold yourself together. You have the energy to live your life. You have the energy to become physically fit. You have the energy you need to expand the harmony between your psychological self and your physical self. When you exercise your personality you feel more able and willing to exercise your body.

The Four Keys
to Psychological Fitness

When you are exercising your personality, or mind jogging, you have four basic personality responses: your expression increases, your activity increases, your clarity or awareness increases, and your level of feeling increases. The better shape you are in psychologically, the more effectively you are able to use these four personality dynamics. When these dynamics are low, it means your personality is not working up to its potential, so you have more problems than solutions, more negative experiences than positive ones. It is the same as getting easily exhausted when you exercise because you are out of shape.

BRINGING THE INNER SELF AND OUTER SELF TOGETHER: USING THE FOUR KEYS TO PERSONALITY

When you are expressing, you are mind jogging. When you are active, you are mind jogging. When you are clear, you are mind jogging. When you are feeling, you are mind jogging. When you are using all four of these dynamics together fully, then you are harmonizing your inner self with your outer self.

When your four personality dynamics are not functioning up to their potential, you will notice that something is wrong. Most often people identify their outer selves with the parts of their personality that they aren't using. They say things like "I'm just a quiet person," "I've got nothing to say," "I don't feel very much," "I can't say what I feel," "That's too physical for me." Often, you never find out what your real outer self is until you bring your inner self and outer self together. You are never just one or the other. You are both.

Throughout the book we will teach you to use all of your personality dynamics. For, when you use only one or two dynamics, you are out of balance. Your inner self and outer self cannot come together.

FOUR NEW QUESTIONS

In order to understand the four dynamics of your personality ask yourself the following four questions. When you can give positive answers to all four of these questions then you will know what a peak performance is. When you can't give a positive answer, that indicates a personality dynamic that needs to be developed.

1. *How expressive am I?*

   (This means—Do I say what I feel and think? And if I do say it, does it match the intensity with which I feel it? And does it come out the way that I want it to?)

2. *How active am I?*

   (This means—How physically active am I? Do I stand in the background, or do I stand my ground? Am I physically *active* or passive? Am I moving in this situation, or am I frozen?)

3. *How aware or clear am I in this situation?*

   (This means—Do I know what is going on and why?)

4. *How much feeling or emotion do I have?*

    (This means—Do I allow myself to experience all the feelings or emotions that I have, or do I try to keep my emotions buried?)

If you are high in two or three of these dynamics and low in the others, this tells you which dynamic you need to change to cope with situations more effectively. When the dynamics are unbalanced, you are not using your potential fully or effectively.

If you are low in all of these dynamics you are not mind jogging at all. You are at a psychological standstill. What is happening on the outside often overwhelms what is happening on the inside. Your inner self doesn't have a chance to reach its potential. You feel separated from what is going on —you are out of control.

The more you try to control the outside situation the more out of control you feel. The paradox of mind jogging is that when you stop trying to control the outside situation and concentrate your efforts on exercising your personality and using all its dynamics fully, then you gain control. You learn how to respond to what *does* happen. Mind jogging is the practice of maximum responding. The more that you are able to respond in a situation up to your full potential the more you will sense that your inner self and outer self match.

In the personality-rating boxes on page 14, rate your outer personality and your ideal or inner personality as you think you are generally. Rate your outer and inner personalities according to the following key:

HIGH: You use this dynamic all the time. You know this is a strength.

MODERATE: You use this dynamic sometimes, but you often forget to keep using it.

LOW: You have more problems than successes with this dynamic. You know this is a weakness for you.

It is easy to understand the concepts of inner self and outer self when you rate your personality dynamics in this way. If your inner personality rates high in expression and your

OUTER PERSONALITY

	Expression	Activity	Clarity	Feeling
High				
Moderate				
Low				

INNER PERSONALITY

	Expression	Activity	Clarity	Feeling
High				
Moderate				
Low				

outer personality rates low, it is not hard to imagine the conflicts that occur internally and the problems that you have externally.

Mike rated himself low in expression for his outer self and high for his inner self. This simple clarification of what was happening inside him changed his negative focus. "I used to think that I had nothing to say, or that what I had to say was unimportant. Or, even worse, that because I had trouble saying things, it meant I was a sick person. I thought that I was lacking some essential cog, or nut, or bolt in my brain. I always thought I would have to live with my inability to express what I thought. During your program I realized that I just didn't have the skills I needed to express what I wanted to express. I never took that viewpoint before—that I had something I wanted to express, but I just didn't know how. I realized the only reason I had trouble was because *I did* have something that I wanted to express. When I began to understand this I went easier on myself. The rest was easy. I just began learning the expressive skills I needed. I can feel it now when what I am expressing and what I want to express come together. I know when I am saying what I have to say."

NEUROSIS VS. LACK OF SKILLS

In the psychological fitness perspective we have found many of the labels of neurosis are outdated. They give you a reason why you are a way you don't want to be. In the fitness perspective we know that each person is doing everything he can to survive. When you don't have the skills you need to do what is good for you, you are often labeled "neurotic," or "sick," or "emotionally disturbed." If you possessed the skills you needed for a better relationship you would use them. If you possessed the skills you needed to feel better you would use them. We have found that the very awareness that you have "something wrong" is the beginning of a solution.

Many people become very confused about their inner selves and outer selves. Gail was beautiful. Everyone told her so. She didn't feel like a beauty—she felt more like a blob. We asked Gail to rate her activity dynamic for her outer self and her inner self. She said, "My outer self is a slug. This I rate really, really low. But I see my inner self as being very active; like I used to be when I was eight or nine. Now I feel frozen and ugly." Once Gail began mind jogging, her understanding of her personality dynamics changed.

"I used to keep changing friends and boyfriends. I wanted them to keep telling me I was beautiful. In fact, no one could ever tell me enough to make me feel beautiful. Finally, I learned to reach for the potential of my inner self. I never thought of it that way. I never took the time to think about how I wanted to be and to reach for that. I just kept thinking of how I wasn't. A lot of times during sex, I would get excited and wanted to do something, but I didn't know what to do. I felt held in. Then I learned how to begin taking action. It really was a new skill. I was taught how to be active again. The more active I became the better I felt. I actually started to feel beautiful. It was hard for me to keep remembering that I didn't have to move and be active—but that I already had that much movement and activity inside of me. I just needed to learn the skill of putting what I had into action. It sounds simple—until it's you trying to learn the skill. I felt like a moose. Now I feel like a gazelle."

To find out who you are, you need to experience yourself in action. You can't sit down and figure yourself out. Who you are is the secret of your inner self. As you learn how to unlock that secret you will stop trying to become someone else. You can begin enjoying who you really are.

The action of mind jogging helps you to become clearer about yourself. Sometimes your outer self is not clear about what is going on in the outer world, so your outer actions come in conflict with your inner clarity. What you think about yourself and what the world thinks are "worlds apart."

Don is a perfect example. Don loved to paint. He never sold any pictures and lived off a small inheritance. His inner self was very clear about what he wanted and what he knew. But his outer self was totally confused about the way the world functioned. He rated his inner clarity dynamic high and his outer clarity dynamic low. He would often complain that "the world doesn't understand me." As he began to see the discrepancy between his inner clarity and his outer clarity, he stopped waiting for the world to understand him. "I used to think I would be discovered. Hell, I hadn't taken the time to discover that I couldn't understand anything that lay beyond the end of a paint brush. The more that I learned about getting clearer the more clear I became. I stopped separating myself from the world. I stopped pitting me against the world."

We asked you to rate your inner clarity and outer clarity because many people never take the time to find out the difference between the two. Actually, when one is high and the other low—your overall clarity is out of balance. You have a distorted view of the world. As you learn to mind jog, your inner clarity leads to more outer clarity and your outer clarity leads to more inner clarity.

Look at your inner rating for feeling and compare it to your outer rating. In our culture most people say they have more feeling on the inside than they do on the outside. But very few have the skills to use that inner feeling. People believe that feelings occur when an outside situation is so powerful that the feelings just gush out.

George was like that. He was a successful salesman. "I used to think that the only time I felt anything was when I would watch an old sad movie. My wife would often be asleep, and I would be sitting in bed watching all the old stars. Each one had his or her own way of breaking my heart. I would look for my favorites. I rated myself high in inner feeling but low in outer feeling. It took me some time to realize that I had outer feelings all the time. I just didn't know it. The more that I learned how to be aware of and use my feelings moment to moment, the more I noticed how seldom other people seemed to do it. I use my feelings now to help me. I can feel myself—I can feel it when my client is afraid or nervous; and instead of avoiding it, I talk directly to the feelings."

George, Don, Gail, and Mike all rated themselves high in one personality dynamic for their inner self and low in the same dynamic for their outer self. There are any number of possible combinations of ratings. That is why there are so many different kinds of personalities. Each personality will obviously have some strengths that are greater than the rest. But each of you can learn to use all of your personality dynamics. If you do not, you are out of balance, and aren't working up to your potential. You will always have an excuse for having troubles.

Mind jogging will not take away all the situations in your life that are troublesome or problematic, but it will increase your ability to respond to each situation with your full personality potential. As you exercise, your inner and outer selves will come together through the use of your personality dynamics.

YOUR TOTAL PERSONALITY:
HOW THE FOUR PERSONALITY DYNAMICS
WORK TOGETHER

You know when you are exercising because you can feel your-self taking action with each of the four personality dynamics. When you have developed each of the four dynamics, your inner self knows that you have the potential to do more, and your outer self knows how to do it. Your outer self knows what your inner self wants to do, and your outer self learns to use all of the personality dynamics to do it.

Mind jogging is using your personality fully. As soon as you begin taking the action of learning how to develop your personality dynamics you are becoming psychologically fit. You have found the system that is the solution to your problems.

One of the best places to start getting more fit is in situa-tions where you think there is nothing left to do—situations where you think you will have to "wait it out." A man told us this story.

"My father had a serious heart problem and was going in for major heart surgery. He was scheduled to leave, and he didn't tell me until two hours before he was to catch his plane for the heart clinic in Texas. I told him I would meet him at the airport. When I first saw him my stomach tightened up. I felt mad at him for not letting me know sooner. We sat down in the waiting area. The first thing that I said was 'Why didn't you tell me sooner?' I knew what the answer would be: 'I didn't want to worry you.' We talked and half argued for twenty minutes. And then it hit me—my dad could die. I looked at him and said, 'Dad, I'm scared for you, you might die. I'm so tired of all our stupid little fights. I never tell you how much I love you. I want you to know that—I love you!' I had tears in my eyes. I felt my stomach relax. Then my father said, 'It's not so bad. I'll be OK.' I couldn't believe what I was hearing. My entire life he had talked like he was a living pyramid, as if he had no highs or lows, no feelings, no fears. I almost decided to shut up and go on the way we had been going on for years. I was getting ready to try and convince him with an argument. But instead I just blurted out, 'Dad, I'm scared. I love you but I can't understand how you can go on talking this way. You have more than one kind of heart trouble. You could die, you're not a stone.'

" 'I think I better get on the plane, son. I need to find my seat.' I just couldn't let him do this. 'Dad, you have a few minutes left with me.' I grabbed him by his arms. He was always small, but now as his health failed him his arms seemed fragile and brittle. I held him close to me and cried. 'Dad, I love you. I'm worried about you. I want you to live. I want you to know how much I love you.'

"He pulled away from me and walked toward the loading door. Then he turned. He was crying. He came over to me and held my face. 'David, I love you, too. I'm not a stone. I am scared, son. I've never been so scared in all my life. Oh God, I'm scared. I don't have a stone heart. I do love you.' "

There was nothing either of these men could do about the serious heart trouble of the father. What was wrong was beyond their control, but how they were in this situation was in their control. As they changed how they were in the situation they were mind jogging. They started expressing, taking action, being clearer, and feeling more with each other. They stopped giving each other excuses and reasons for keeping their inner selves out of harmony with their outer selves.

Once you understand this way of looking at emotional problems you have a whole new perspective on your life. You will stop trying to remove all the problems from your life, which is impossible, and start looking at how you respond to your problems. Then your problems become just problems and not unsolvable crises.

To help you understand how the personality works let's analyze this last example. The son showed a fit response to the situation because he was using all of his personality dynamics up to their potential.

In that way we could say that his inner self and his outer self were matched. He felt good about what he did, he understood why he did it. But the father's inner self was different from his outer self. His inner self had more expression, more activity, more clarity, and more feeling than he was showing.

SON'S RATINGS FOR
BOTH INNER AND OUTER SELF

	Expression	Activity	Clarity	Feeling
High	X	X	X	X
Moderate	X	X	X	X
Low	X	X	X	X

The father's outer self had low expression, low activity, low clarity, and low feeling. He probably was thinking something like this: "I feel very sad. I am so glad that David is talking to me." But all of this expression was going on in his head. Once David confronted his father, his father thought, "I knew this might happen" (low clarity), "I am going to leave"

FATHER'S INNER SELF

	Expression	Activity	Clarity	Feeling
High	X	X	X	X
Moderate	X	X	X	X
Low	X	X	X	X

FATHER'S OUTER SELF

	Expression	Activity	Clarity	Feeling
High				
Moderate				
Low	X	X	X	X

(low activity). In some ways the dramatic situation of the heart trouble and his son talking to him had allowed the father to find his inner self. He had a sense of what could be if he took new psychological action.

FATHER'S MIND JOG

	Expression	Activity	Clarity	Feeling
High			X	X
Moderate	X	X	X	X
Low	X	X	X	X

The father's personality dynamics changed as he allowed his inner self and outer self to blend. He didn't have the skills to maximize his inner and outer selves, but he was beginning. When the father turned back to his son, he stopped being just his outer self. As the father responded to his son he was chancing that awkward feeling that comes with starting any new behavior. He wasn't sure of what he was going to do or how to do it right, but he did it—that is what mind jogging feels like. The father's stretch toward a new way of being brought his inner and outer selves together.

3

The Fifth Key: Contact

The fifth personality dynamic—contact—is the one that helps the others happen. Mind jogging is a contact sport. As you learn the skills of expression, activity, clarity, and feeling, your contact increases. Every person you come into contact with becomes a new teammate, someone who makes your mind jogging more complete, more complex, and more satisfying.

Often people come to us seeking to learn different skills. They think they want to master a personality skill like aggressive expression, or orgasmic sexuality, or happy feelings. They don't know that psychological fitness involves all five personality dynamics.

Gene came to one of our fitness programs because he wanted to be more successful. Though he read *Fortune Magazine,* shopped for the latest fashions, and drove a white Cadillac Seville, he was one of the most dismal failures who had ever come into our programs. He told us, "I want to learn to relax—you know, the 'dynamic relaxation' that you lecture about. I want to be able to be more relaxed so I can work more. I know where I am going, and I want to get there in the best way possible." He already had the possessions that many people want—or think they want. Unfortunately, he had nothing the moment he stopped working. He had divorced his wife because she wanted too much of his time. He had no friends. He didn't know it but he was headed for psychological disaster. We asked him where he thought he was going. He looked at us as if we were the most naive people in the world. "Don't you know the name of the game? It's success. I'm going to the top."

The first step in teaching Gene how to begin mind jogging was to get him to stop running. He thought that getting to the top meant eliminating all the people in his life. He was wrong. Material success alone isn't success at all. Success exists only if it is shared. Gene couldn't slow down because then he would have had to face how lonely he was.

Contact is perhaps the most powerful of the personality dynamics. We have been trying to teach you about contact with yourself, the harmonizing of your inner and outer selves. Of course this involves making contact with people in the world around you. Each person you have in your life provides the opportunity to use all the different personality skills. The more effective you are in using your personality dynamics with other people the easier it will be to make contact. You will begin having friends who are lifetime friends, you will have loves that last for years, strangers will be accessible, and your inner and outer bonds will grow stronger. You will become surer of who you are and who are the people around you.

At its most basic level, contact means being around people. People need people. In all our work, we have found that when people have a sense of security and love with other people, they relax, their natural talents come to the surface, their wounds are more easily healed, and what cannot be healed is accepted and integrated.

CONTACT AND THERAPY

A recent research article reported on 2,000 young people suffering from the first episode of acute psychosis. They were treated with supportive therapy, chemicals, institutions, and restraints. A ten-year follow-up revealed that the last three may not be necessary and are often harmful due to the many side effects. Supportive therapy provided the contact these young patients needed to increase their fitness.

We think that much of psychology and psychiatry has overlooked those natural behaviors that heal us and keep us healthy. Contact with good friends and contact with your family is important to your psychological fitness. Many values like family, friends, and community have been lost in our rush to modernize ourselves. But this rush left us without the tools we need to fight psychological diseases. People with few friends tend to have higher physical symptom levels and have a greater number of self-related threatening events. Contact needs to be reinstated as a psychological necessity. As simple as it seems, we keep forgetting that we need friends and that our friends need us.

BABIES NEED CONTACT

The psychiatrist Rene Spitz studied what happened to infants who during the ages six months to twelve months had had to be separated from their mothers and put into institutions or foster homes. In the substitute homes the infants received adequate food and care, but busy nurses or foster parents could do very little mothering. During the first three to four weeks the infants became easily upset, cried a lot, lost weight, and had trouble sleeping. After that the babies withdrew and became very passive and quiet. They would not play and became more susceptible to colds and other illnesses. Mortality rates increased very sharply. Spitz comments, "The deprivation of emotional supplies, at least in the period of early infancy, is a destructive stressor agent."

We can give you statistics about contact, what it means and how much we need it, but you must ultimately decide that contact makes psychological sense to you. You must take the action necessary to get the contact you need.

A MINI-EXERCISE

Bet a friend or your family a dinner that you can make them all feel better in just fifteen minutes a day. The trick we want you to use is to turn off the TV for fifteen minutes a day and talk. Sit and visit. Turn off the radio, take the phone off the hook. The only trouble you will have is deciding where to go for dinner. This exercise is going to put you face to face with your ability to make contact. The people you ask to stop watching TV are going to give you reasons for doing it later, or tell you that you are nuts. But if you insist, it is like getting them out jogging—once you do, everyone will feel better. It takes strength, but test yourself and see if you can do it.

CONTACT AND INDEPENDENCE

A widespread misconception exists that "really together" people are completely independent and self-sufficient. Though some individuals work better by themselves and become great artists or inventors or scientists or athletes, no one can become psychologically fit by himself. The fit person is not a superman or superwoman who does not need or depend upon people.

There is another basic misconception about contact. It goes something like this—"I know some people who aren't dependent on anyone else." It is a basic fact that people today are dependent on people they don't even know—farmers, water engineers, fishermen, ranchers, truck drivers, policemen, and power company workers. The more contact that we make with the people we depend upon the better we feel.

Contact does more than insure that we survive the onslaughts of the environment. It guarantees us better physical and mental health. It makes our life better.

Breakdown or Breakthrough

If contact is necessary for psychological and physical fitness, and it *is*, then what are the characteristics of good personal contact? And what happens when it is increased or decreased?

Good contact makes you feel good. In order to increase it you must develop the four dynamics of your personality to their greatest potential. That means you have to have high expression, high activity, high clarity, and high feeling. When your personality is functioning at its maximum, you make contact breakthroughs.

A contact breakthrough gives you new insight into your own behavior, your own personality and development. You begin trusting yourself and other people more. Your inner sense of contact and caring is matched by your outer skills of contact and caring. You are no longer alone.

When contact decreases, you are heading toward a breakdown. The more you decrease any of the personality dynamics the more your contact decreases. There is no such thing as mental disease—there is only disuse. A breakdown occurs when you stop using your personality dynamics.

If you find yourself in a situation in which your contact is breaking down, look first at how you are using your personality dynamics. Don't worry about the content or why the situation is occurring. Pay attention to how well your personality is or isn't working, and do something about that before you try to change the situation. After you take care of yourself, you will have a clearer perspective on what to do with the situation (if anything still needs to be done!).

THE TWO T'S OF CONTACT

The basic skills of emotional education are "touching" and "talking"; they are as basic and important for psychological fitness as are the three R's for intellectual fitness.

Without touching and talking you cannot exercise your personality, and without psychological exercise you cannot stay fit.

CONTACT AND HEALTH

Dr. Lisa Berkman, a research specialist with the Human Population Lab of the California Department of Public Health, did an analysis of the relationship between mortality rates and social ties. She analyzed data on 7,000 adults who were followed for nine years and found that people who have few social contacts are 2½ to 3 times more likely to die prematurely than those with a more active social life. Social contacts predicted mortality rates independent of health practices such as smoking and obesity.

Dr. James Lynch, scientific director of the Psychosomatic Clinics at the University of Maryland School of Medicine, commented on these results by advising, "People have to learn to take human relationships as seriously as they do exercise and diet. We would be healthier if we had more social contacts."

Touching: The First Basic Contact Exercise

To begin to be more psychologically fit you can take a very important first step. Make sure that you are touched today.

There are many ways you can be touched. You can be touched both physically and emotionally. Both are vitally important. In your daily routine physically touch your own face and body more. Touch your friends as you talk to them. If you increase your touching by 10 percent you will find you have a 10 percent energy increase in all your other personality dynamics. Physical touching makes it possible to have emotional touching. The more you use touching the more you will develop all the other dynamics of your personality.

Talking: The Second Basic Contact Exercise

Talking and touching are as basic to psychological fitness as moving and stretching are to physical fitness. Without talking you cannot fully exercise your personality dynamics. You need talking to develop your contact.

A study by the Soviet Institute of Gerontology in Moscow

found that one factor that is common to people who live past the age of a hundred is that none of them are lazy. All of them work hard and "talk a lot."

We have met many young people who work hard and who will be lucky to live past fifty. All of their talk is confined to work. They are able to make shop talk but not personal talk.

If we could teach children one basic psychological fitness skill we would teach them how to talk about themselves. Most young children are eager to talk, but as they grow up they learn to talk more and more about objects and less and less about themselves. Talking about objects keeps a distance between your inner self and outer self. Your talking needs to blend how you feel, what you are doing, and what you think. When you learn how to *talk* and make contact, you have a new freedom—a new way to communicate. You are no longer restricted to conversations that go nowhere when you run out of "things" to say.

CONTACT RESEARCH

One research investigation reported in the *American Journal of Psychiatry* showed that as most children get older they begin to describe their feelings as ideas and thoughts rather than as body sensations. Children literally become "out of touch" with their own feelings. As adults they are unable to contact other adults. They can talk *about* their feelings in the same way that they talk about work and food and current events, but they cannot *express their feelings.*

Another very fascinating line of recent research shows that normal human beings who are talking together enter into an unconscious pattern of synchronized movements, a "sort of dance." This dance of contact when talking is only observable using a frame-by-frame analysis of filmed interactions.

Dr. William Condon, the discoverer of this phenomenon, also observed that autistic children are not able to maintain the smooth micro-movements in response to conversation: they show "jerks and jumps." The mothers of autistic children are much more likely to show histories of "family discord," breaks in healthy contact during their pregnancies. The distress the mothers experience seems to be communicated directly to their unborn children through neuroendocrinal changes in blood transmitted from the mother to the fetus. Contact loss therefore has its effects even before birth.

How to Talk

We suggest that many people in this country need a course in remedial talking. Lots of attention has been paid to "Why Johnny can't read" but little attention to "Why Johnny can't talk." The answers are similar. Johnny doesn't read very well because the people around him don't read very much or very well. Johnny doesn't express his feelings very well because the people around him don't.

One of the leading authorities on physical fitness, Dr. Lawrence Morehouse, wrote an excellent book in which he stated that people could maintain *Total Fitness in 30 Minutes a Day*. We believe that it would be possible for most people to maintain total psychological fitness with thirty minutes of personal talking a day.

For many people thirty minutes of personal talking will be a 300 percent increase, and they will need to work up to it gradually, going from one to five minutes and then from ten to fifteen to twenty to thirty. Each increment will be experienced as a big change in your life. If you want to find out how long five minutes of personal talking really is, try to talk aloud to yourself, right now, for five minutes. It's a long time.

In Part 2 we will help you learn contact skills. For now you can understand Principle Four intellectually.

PRINCIPLE FOUR: Fitness cannot be attained or maintained without contact.

Contact is maintained by touching and talking. Contact brings together and harmonizes our basic personality dynamics.

OTHER SOCIETIES

Our society emphasizes academic and work skills, not contact skills. But there are societies where social skills are as carefully and lengthily taught as arithmetic and reading.

The Fore of New Guinea were carefully studied by Dr. Richard Sorenson, who is director of the Smithsonian National Anthropological Film Center. He reports, "Theirs was a way of life different from anything I had seen or heard about before. . . . A responsive sixth sense seemed to attune the Fore hamlet mates to each other's interests and needs. . . . Subtle, even fleeting expressions of interest, desire and discomfort were quickly read and helpfully acted on by one's associates. This spontaneous urge to share food, affection, work, trust, tools and pleasure was the social cement that held the Fore hamlets together. It was a pleasant way of life, for one could always be with those with whom one got along well."

In an article entitled "Somebody Else Should Be Your Own Best Friend," the anthropologist Dr. Robert Brain describes the close contacts in the Bangwa society of western Africa. "These non-western people placed great emphasis on the value of friendship between two persons not related by kinship or sexual attachment. . . . At first I was taken aback by their fervent, demonstrative attitudes toward friends . . . but I had little choice and eventually learned how to be a best friend, by, for example, verbalizing affection, giving gifts, and accompanying friends on journeys." The Bangwa were more skilled than Dr. Brain at contact, and they taught him skills in which he had never been formally instructed.

When society moved at a slower pace there was more time for conversation. But though we don't live in a slow-paced society we still need the skills of contact—talking and touching—if we are to survive. Many people who live alone leave the television on just to hear voices. They are trying to make electronic contact, not knowing they need people for contact. It is becoming increasingly clear that contact is vital for our psychophysiological survival.

Within ten years the research on contact, disease, and stress will change many of the ideas now current in medicine and psychology. The best medicine for people is people. Contact is the fifth key to understanding the personality, and it is the secret of mind jogging. Mind jogging helps you make contact. We can promise you that as you learn to mind jog you will learn to talk, to touch, to hear, to see, to love, to eat, to sleep, and to dream with satisfaction. You will learn how to really take care of yourself. Contact is more than an extra dimension to our personalities—it is vital to our survival.

How Fit Are You?
Give Yourself a Psychological Checkup

In the checkup you are about to take you will be asked ten questions about your fitness in each of the following ten life areas:

WORK FITNESS	EMOTIONAL FITNESS
PLAY FITNESS	INTELLECTUAL FITNESS
RELATIONSHIP FITNESS	PHYSICAL FITNESS
LOVE FITNESS	MORAL FITNESS
SEX FITNESS	SLEEP AND DREAM FITNESS

Your answers to these questions should help you find out in just what areas you are strong and in what areas you are weak. You will have a clearer idea of where your mind jogging needs to begin.

Right now, before you take the tests, just guess what you will score in each area.

After you have taken the tests, compare your actual scores to the guesses.

"GUESS CHECKUP"

Guess how you will rate in each of the following areas. The weakness range goes from 1-3, with 1 being the weakest. If an area is a weakness, place a mark in one of the first three boxes. The "in-between" range is 4-7, with 4 tending toward weakness and 7 tending toward strength. For areas in which you don't feel particularly weak or strong, place a mark in one of these four boxes. The strength range is 8-10, with 10 being the strongest. Use these three boxes to mark your strengths.

	Work	Play	Relation-ships	Love	Sexual	Emotional	Intellectual	Physical	Moral	Sleep & Dreams
10										
9										
8										
7										
6										
5										
4										
3										
2										
1										

You don't have to be a psychologist to give yourself a psychological checkup any more than you need to be a physician to check your own height, weight, pulse, and temperature. The purpose of this checkup is to identify your areas of psychological strength. We expect it will both help you feel better and teach you what to do next to help yourself. We hope you will find that the questions you answer "no" to will give you new insight into what strengths you have the potential to develop.

WORK FITNESS

		YES	NO
1.	In general, do you enjoy working?	——	——
2.	Are you financially successful, according to your own standards, in your work?	——	——
3.	Are you successfully pursuing your chosen career?	——	——
4.	Are your work skills improving?	——	——
5.	Do you work well alone?	——	——
6.	Do you work well with others?	——	——
7.	Do you have a positive opinion of the way you work?	——	——
8.	Do you have a positive opinion of your potential to work?	——	——
9.	Have your attitudes about work improved, compared to earlier times in your life?	——	——
10.	Do you have the skills you need to work as successfully as you want to work?	——	——
	TOTALS	——	——

PLAY FITNESS

		YES	NO
1.	Do you enjoy sports?	—	—
2.	Do you enjoy playing household games (cards, box games, etc.)?	—	—
3.	Do you enjoy participating in competitive play?	—	—
4.	Do you enjoy participating in noncompetitive play?	—	—
5.	Do you play well with others?	—	—
6.	Do you play three times or more a week?	—	—
7.	Do you have a positive opinion of yourself as a player?	—	—
8.	Do you have the skills you need to play as well as you want to play?	—	—
9.	Do you play as much as you want?	—	—
10.	Has your *satisfaction* with your play increased, compared to earlier times in your life?	—	—
	TOTALS	—	—

RELATIONSHIP FITNESS

		YES	NO
1.	Do you enjoy your friendships?	—	—
2.	Do you trust and depend on your friends when you need someone to lean on?	—	—
3.	Do your friends trust and depend on you when they need someone to lean on?	—	—
4.	Do you see friends regularly (at least three times a week)?	—	—

5. Do you have close friends of both sexes? ___ ___

6. Do you have long-term friendships (of three years or more)? ___ ___

7. Do you have a positive opinion of your ability to make and keep friends? ___ ___

8. Do other people have a positive opinion of your ability to make and keep friends? ___ ___

9. Are you satisfied with your friendships? ___ ___

10. Do you have the skills you need to make and keep as many friends as you want? ___ ___

                                    TOTALS ___ ___

LOVE FITNESS   YES   NO

1. Do you enjoy making physical contact with your lover? ___ ___

2. Are you good friends with your lover? ___ ___

3. Do you share your secret thoughts with your lover? ___ ___

4. Do you share your intimate feelings with your lover? ___ ___

5. Have you ever had a long-term love relationship (three years or more)? ___ ___

6. Do you have a positive opinion of your present ability to love? ___ ___

7. Do other people have a positive opinion of your ability to love? ___ ___

8. Are you satisfied with your love relationship? ___ ___

9. Do you have the interpersonal skills you need to have a love relationship? ___ ___

10. Do you have a positive opinion of your potential to love? —— ——

TOTALS —— ——

SEXUAL FITNESS   YES   NO

1. Do you enjoy sex? —— ——

2. Do you have sex as often as you want? —— ——

3. Do you usually express your secret thoughts during sex? —— ——

4. Do you usually express your intimate feelings during sex? —— ——

5. Do you have the sexual skills to do what you want to do during sex? —— ——

6. Do you have sex regularly (at least three times a week)? —— ——

7. Do you have a positive opinion of your sexual life? —— ——

8. Do other people have a positive opinion of your sexual life? —— ——

9. Have your attitudes about sex improved, compared to earlier times in your life? —— ——

10. Are you satisfied with all aspects of your sex life? —— ——

TOTALS —— ——

EMOTIONAL FITNESS   YES   NO

1. Can you express anger easily? —— ——

2. Can you express sadness easily? —— ——

3. Can you express happiness easily? ___ ___

4. Can you express fear easily? ___ ___

5. Do you express your emotions to others easily and freely? ___ ___

6. Do you use your emotions to help you to make your decisions? ___ ___

7. Do you have a positive opinion of your potential to be emotional? ___ ___

8. Do you have a positive opinion of the way you are using your present emotional skills? ___ ___

9. Are those around you as emotional as you want? ___ ___

10. Do you have the skills you need to be as emotional as you want to be? ___ ___

TOTALS ___ ___

INTELLECTUAL FITNESS   YES   NO

1. Do you *enjoy* thinking and solving problems? ___ ___

2. Are your intellectual skills improving? ___ ___

3. Do you share your ideas and thoughts with others? ___ ___

4. Do you learn easily? ___ ___

5. Do you have the skills you need in order to be as intellectual as you want to be? ___ ___

6. Do you think creatively? ___ ___

7. Do you have a positive opinion of the way you use your present intellectual skills?

8. Do other people have a positive opinion of your intellectual abilities? ___ ___

9. Do you have a positive opinion of your potential to be intellectual? ___ ___

10. Are you satisfied with your intellectual abilities? ___ ___

TOTALS ___ ___

PHYSICAL FITNESS

YES NO

1. Is your physical fitness improving? ___ ___

2. Are you a good weight for your age and health? ___ ___

3. Do you have physical vitality, an energetic, healthy presence? ___ ___

4. Are you physically flexible and supple? ___ ___

5. Do you have a positive opinion of your potential to be physically fit? ___ ___

6. Do others have a good opinion of your physical fitness? ___ ___

7. Are you well coordinated? ___ ___

8. Are you satisfied with the way you are using your present fitness skills? ___ ___

9. Have your physical fitness attitudes improved, compared to earlier times in your life? ___ ___

10. Do you have the skills you need to be as fit as you want to be? ___ ___

TOTALS ___ ___

MORAL FITNESS   YES   NO

1. Are you trustworthy?   ___   ___

2. Do you take responsibility for your
    actions?   ___   ___

3. Are you more moral and ethical than at
    earlier times in your life?   ___   ___

4. Are you honest?   ___   ___

5. Are you fair and just?   ___   ___

6. Do you respect the moral values of
    others?   ___   ___

7. Is your moral code flexible?   ___   ___

8. Do you have a positive opinion of your
    moral and ethical beliefs and behavior?   ___   ___

9. Do other people have a positive opinion
    of your moral and ethical beliefs and be-
    havior?   ___   ___

10. Are you satisfied with your own moral
    and ethical behavior?   ___   ___

                              TOTALS   ___   ___

SLEEP AND DREAM FITNESS   YES   NO

1. Do you use your dreams to help yourself
    understand and change your life?   ___   ___

2. Do you have the skills you need to under-
    stand and use your dreams?   ___   ___

3. Are you satisfied with your dream life?   ___   ___

4. Generally, do you feel good in your
    dreams?   ___   ___

5. Do you remember your dreams at least three times a week?   —— ——

6. Do you discuss your dreams with friends and acquaintances at least once a week?   —— ——

7. Do you feel rested and alert upon waking?   —— ——

8. Do you sleep soundly?   —— ——

9. Do you fall asleep easily and naturally without drugs or alcohol?   —— ——

10. Are you satisfied with your sleep fitness?   —— ——

TOTALS   —— ——

How to Interpret and Use Your Score to
Begin Improving Your Psychological Fitness

This is a good time to get yourself a fitness notebook. You'll want something portable that you can make notes in—wherever you are—something in which you can easily write down the answers to the questions we'll be asking you.

SCORING

1. Total all the areas in which you scored 8 or more yeses. (These areas are your strengths.)

2. Total all the areas in which you scored 3 or fewer yeses. (These areas are your weaknesses.)

3. Do you have, overall, more strengths than weaknesses, or more weaknesses than strengths?

4. Notice all of your scores between 8 and 3. These are potential strengths that will quickly become strengths if you pay more attention to them. In Part 2 we will work with these areas.

5. Do the scores of strengths and weaknesses seem to match what you secretly felt about yourself but maybe never took the time to say out loud?

Fill in the total number of yeses scored for each area. In assessing your score, answer the questions on the following page.

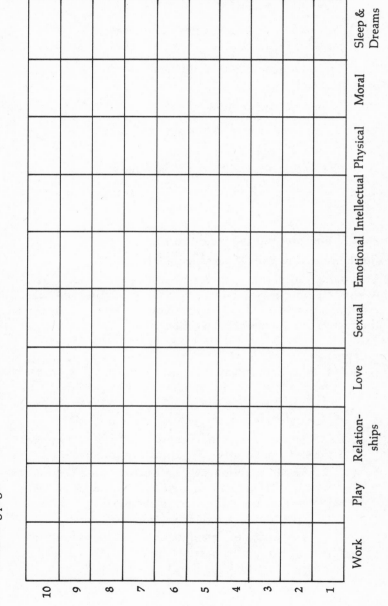

6. Look at each area in which you scored 3 or less. Instead of thinking that you scored low—think about your potential in those areas.

7. Think about how you have changed or not changed in any particular area over the years.

8. Think about how you can change, using your strengths as guides.

9. Think about your weaknesses as muscles that need to be exercised.

10. Think about your strengths as muscles that need to be exercised and stressed to stay fit and become more fit.

11. Think about stressing your entire personality in a safe way so that you can become psychologically fit.

12. Were you satisfied with your scores? Did any scores surprise you?

13. Look at your overall scores. Can you see how you have some strengths and some weaknesses? Think about how they interact with each other to keep your personality at a standstill.

14. Think about what you would be like if all your scores were strengths. What would that do to your self-esteem? What problems are created in your life because of your weaknesses? What are your fears about having a life with no weaknesses?

15. Compare your guess checkup with your real checkup. How close did you come?

HOW IT ALL FITS TOGETHER

You have now taken your "psychological." These ten areas that you have self-evaluated give you a good idea of where you can begin. The next question you need answered is, "How can I begin working on them?" We are not surprised when people are able to guess what they would score in each area accurately. They are often aware of their strengths and weaknesses, but they are not sure how to change.

Connie was a successful model. She was doing nationally

televised commercials. When she went out on a job interview she was a dynamo. She would express, she was active, she was clear, she had lots of positive feeling, and she made contact. When she gave herself the checkup she scored a 10 in work. But she scored a 3 in relationships. When asked about how well her personality functioned in relationships she said, "I don't know what happens, but when I try to get to know somebody on a deeper level, I put my foot in my mouth, I feel immobile, I can't think of anything to do, I feel ghastly inside, and I just can't maintain a relationship." It was clear that she needed to learn how to use her personality in more areas of her life than work.

Connie had trouble allowing her inner self to come out in situations in which she felt vulnerable. Relationships formed the first area in which she began mind jogging.

When you are using all your personality dynamics and you score 10 in a particular area you have a peak performance. Connie scored a peak performance in work. Her score looked like this:

CONNIE'S WORK PERFORMANCE: PEAK

    a. Life Area Score: Work 10 (Total number of yeses)

    b. Personality Dynamics Profile:

	Expression	Activity	Clarity	Feeling	Contact
High	X	X	X	X	X
Moderate	X	X	X	X	X
Low	X	X	X	X	X

Her work performance score was much different from her relationship performance score.

CONNIE'S RELATIONSHIP PERFORMANCE: LOW

    Her less than peak performance looked like this:

    a. Life Area Score: Relationships 3 (Total number of yeses)

b. Personality Dynamics Profile:

High					
Moderate					
Low	X	X	X	X	X
	Expression	Activity	Clarity	Feeling	Contact

Connie knows that the way to a peak performance in relationships is to increase her expression, activity, clarity, feelings, and contact. She doesn't have a problem; she is just facing how few skills she has developed in the area of relationships. Many people think that if they score low in a particular area it means there is something wrong with them. Not so. But it does mean you need to develop skills in particular areas. In Part 2 we will give you step-by-step instructions about developing these skills. Right now we want you to understand how the personality dynamics work in a positive way to help you begin mind jogging.

PEAK PERFORMANCES

Psychologists have been studying peak performances for less than fifty years, and the emphasis has been less on the dynamics of the performance than on the results. We not only want you to attain peak performances with your mind jogging —we want you to know how to continue attaining them. As you come to understand the dynamics of personality your mind jogging will eventually shift from peak performances in a single strength area of your life to maximum performances in many life areas. You will shift your psychological activity and awareness to entirely new levels. Mind jogging changes the valleys or weaknesses of your personality into strengths or peaks.

PART 2

A 21-Day Psychological Fitness Program

5

Getting Started

Psychological fitness means becoming more and enjoying more in your life. Psychological fitness is different from physical fitness because, as you age, you can become more fit than you were in your youth. After all, with age you have had more time for psychological exercising. Fitness means gaining greater flexibility rather than rigidity with age; it means a deeper self-knowledge and greater ability to show who you really are.

We have had many older people in our programs who, through mind jogging, actually became more able to exercise and play than at earlier times in their lives.

To have fun with mind jogging you must recognize that you will never be perfect. If games such as golf and tennis and basketball can never be played to perfection, then most certainly your life will never be lived to perfection. What matters is that you enjoy living and enjoy changing.

The best athletes combine an exquisitely detailed knowledge

of the techniques of their sport with an overall sense of how they feel when playing their best. These two components, technique and feeling, must be developed together.

In the chapters that follow we will give you specific feeling references and guiding images and key thoughts for developing your psychological fitness. These *Feeling* guides, *Image* guides, and *Thought* guides are the backbone of our "F-I-Tness" program. You will also be acquiring an overall sense of fitness—you will learn to feel what is off and what is on. You will acquire both the specific and a general sense of what it is to live in fitness, day by day.

52 WEEKS A YEAR—A FITNESS PHILOSOPHY

Our three-week program is designed to get you started on something you will continue throughout your life.

Mind jogging feels good just as fitness feels good. There is no reason to try to rush through and be done with it. By paying attention to your psychological fitness every day and every week of the year you will be reminding yourself of how good you want to feel. You will not accept a lower standard for yourself than you really want.

It is a worthwhile practice to give yourself a quick psychological checkup daily. Ask yourself this question:

> *What am I going to do today that*
> *will be especially good for me?*

And then, make sure that you put into your day some psychological activity that is certain to make you feel good. If you don't do this you will end up with empty days and empty weeks. You will let the world schedule your life instead of you scheduling what you need and want.

BENJAMIN FRANKLIN
A Philosopher of Psychological Fitness
In his *Memoirs* (1789) and his well-known *Poor Richard's Almanack* (1732–1757) Benjamin Franklin gave timely

advice for using psychological strengths and changing psychological weaknesses. Franklin was an ingenious and practical man who recognized that his feelings and habits could work for him or against him. He described his personal method for changing. "I made a little book in which I allotted a page for each of the virtues. I ruled each page with red ink so as to have seven columns, one for each day of the week, marking each column with a letter for the day . . . I might mark by a little black spot every fault I found upon examination to have been committed respecting that virtue upon that day. I determined to give a week's strict attention to each of the virtues successively. . . . Thus if in the first week I could keep my first line marked 'Temperance' clear of spots, I supposed the habit of that virtue so much strengthened and its opposite weakened that I might venture extending my attention to include the next."

Franklin also described some of the difficulties he encountered. "I was surprised to find myself so much fuller of faults than I had imagined, but I had the satisfaction of seeing them diminish."

When you begin this three-week program, you, like Ben Franklin, must focus not on the number of weaknesses you have but on seeing your weaknesses diminish and your strengths grow. Remember that you want to do mind jogging throughout your lifetime because fitness feels good.

HOW TO USE THE PROGRAM

The three consecutive weeks of exercise in the following three chapters are just a beginning. We want you to make these fitness exercises part of your life. Our method is one that works over time. It will begin to work for you the first day, and by the end of the three weeks you will know how to continue on your own.

As you use the program, be guided by your feelings. If you feel the need to repeat, do so before going on. Work through the entire three weeks at your own pace. The three weeks of guided exercises will give you a specific overview of what we mean by psychological fitness and help you to know what to do whenever you want to develop any special area on your own.

The twenty-one-day program gives you techniques for many different kinds of mind jogging. We added the explanations because psychological fitness is a revolutionary idea in applied psychology, challenging the common notion that people must adjust to their problems and weaknesses and accept themselves as they are. We say, "Become who you can become—don't just stay the way you are."

In Part 1 we discussed ideas about inner selves and outer selves. Often your outer self has become so comfortable with a particular unfit behavior that you will feel awkward as you do one of our exercises. *Awkwardness means that you are trying something new.* It is that very trying which is the process of psychological fitness. Trying new things is a basic skill of mind jogging. It is difficult to give up familiar ways of doing things no matter how unfit they are—unless the new way is more pleasurable. Your unfit behaviors don't disappear, you just stop using them.

Just as you need space for physical jogging (the top of a building, a track, a park, the beach, a green strip along a road) so too do you need psychological space for mind jogging. You create space by giving yourself opportunities to be different. The desire you feel for something new, better, and more exciting is your basic desire for psychological fitness. We don't have to give that desire (we couldn't); you already have it inside yourself.

Each specific exercise has its own meaning. We want to teach you a new understanding and acceptance of yourself. An exercise may not make a great deal of sense at first, but you'll discover that it has been designed like a friendly time bomb. Later in your life it will go off in your head, and you will notice that you have a new skill.

What to Do When You Complete the Program

You will have taken twenty-one major steps toward psychological fitness. You will know many new skills, and you will have a new level of self-awareness about your personality and your life.

Make plans to continue mind jogging. Each week, choose one of the five personality dynamics and one of the ten life areas, and spend at least thirty minutes a day talking and doing exercises that will apply your old strengths and build up new strengths. Use the format we will teach you: warm-up exercises, testing yourself, stretching exercises, building-up exercises, and instant replays. Also, develop your own F-I-T guides.

On some days, throw out all the guides and exercises, and return to basic mind jogging, which is just talking closely and personally about yourself with a friend. You will learn that this twenty-one-day program has made basic mind jogging much easier to do.

If, at the end of any day, you can answer yes to these two questions you will know that you have done at least the minimum amount of mind jogging needed to keep your personality in good shape:

Have I paid attention to how I feel today?

Have I talked closely and personally with a friend today?

Keep in mind that mind jogging is a help to living; it is not your whole life. If, when doing some of the exercises, you find they are taking too much time, cut them back. The purpose of mind jogging is to exercise your personality so you can live better and have more in your life. Don't substitute jogging for living.

We can assure you that if you exercise your personality by mind jogging thirty minutes a day four or five days a week, you will feel the benefits.

Week One:
Stretching Your Personality

Your applied mind jogging starts here. We are going to teach you how to stretch your personality, how to become stronger, and how to begin experiencing peak performances.

We suggest you first read through this section quickly, go on to finish the book, and then come back and do the exercises systematically over a three-week period.

Just as with physical exercises, you are going to make up dozens of excuses for not doing some exercises on some days. Those excuses are your weaknesses speaking to you. Don't listen to them.

The first week's exercises are made to loosen you up and get your personality working.

Remember, psychological fitness has to be practiced and maintained just like physical fitness. No one becomes physically fit once and then stops. Physical fitness requires that you keep active to remain in shape. Psychological fitness is exactly the same. The benefits are twofold: It feels good to get into shape, and it feels good to stay in good psychological shape. You can reach for your peak whenever you want. You aren't afraid to break barriers and try new behaviors. And your daily feeling level is high. You have a sense of well-being. You finally feel the way you have always wanted to feel and know how you can keep it.

AN OVERVIEW OF THE ENTIRE PROGRAM

The program is designed as a twenty-one-day program if you follow it sequentially. But it can also be thought of as twenty-one steps to psychological fitness. Each of the days or steps is designed to have specific as well as overall results. Here is an overview.

Each day will help you feel better and will teach you things that will help you later on. The main thing about this psychological fitness program is that it works. If you follow what we suggest you will find yourself changing. We included the weekends as part of our program so that you can use them for review, for creating new exercises for yourself, or to concentrate on a special area.

Fitness Notebook

You'll need a fitness notebook or diary to keep notes and records in. The next twenty-one days of your life should be some of the most exciting emotional, psychological, and intellectual times you have ever spent. Freely jot down ideas, feelings, and things you notice related to your fitness program. Before you start any of the exercises, write down some of your personal goals, areas you want help with, and problems that you want to solve.

For example:

> I'd like to be more confident at work.
> I'd like to be more positively aggressive
>   in relationships.
> I want to feel better.
> I want to be more financially successful.

	Monday	Tuesday	Wednesday	Thursday	Friday	Weekend
Week One	Expression Exercises	Activity Exercises	Feeling Exercises	Awareness Exercises	Contact Exercises	REST & PLAY
Week Two	Work Exercises	Play Exercises	Relation-ship Exercises	Love Exercises	Sex Exercises	
Week Three	Emotional Fitness Exercises	Intellectual Fitness Exercises	Physical Fitness Exercises	Moral Fitness Exercises	Sleep & Dream Fitness Exercises	

It is important to realize that you need to do just what feels right to you. Take your time—change the exercises so they feel just right to you. Whatever you do—be persistent and consistent.

Remember, these exercises are not intended to embarrass you or put you in a situation that is too trying for you. If you think a particular exercise is not right for you, *don't do it.* But distinguish between an exercise that is not right and an exercise which stretches your personality and gives you a lot of feeling.

The first week's exercises are longer than the other two because they provide an important foundation and help loosen up your personality. In Weeks Two and Three we will help you build up your personality and improve your psychological endurance. The first week we will teach you the basic personality skills which you will use to overcome problems and to develop other life areas.

WEEK ONE/DAY ONE:
EXPRESSION EXERCISES

Today we want to teach you about your level of expression, your beliefs about expression, what limitations you place on expression, and how it can work for you.

Warming Up

Think of your very closest friend. Take the time to imagine how he looks and how much you feel about him. And then let yourself realize that someday he is going to die. You are there with him. What are all the things you will want to say? What feelings would you have? What things would you want to say that you never would have said?

These questions don't tell you how to change—remember, this is just a warm-up. They are designed to get you thinking about your strengths and weaknesses and the skills you need to develop to change your weaknesses into strengths. You will be surprised at how many of these exercises we use now will make sense in your everyday life. All of a sudden you will say, "Oh, that is a strength," or "That is a weakness." What you believe is possible now is often limited by what you have been taught to express or not express. Think about that—what you believe about how you express, what you express, and what is right to express may be directly related to the skills or lack of skills you have in this area.

Understanding your expression warm-up exercise. Answer these questions in your notebook about this warm-up exercise:

1. Is expression a personality strength for you? It might be if you could imagine really talking to your friend, telling your deepest feelings and thoughts. Or is expression a weakness for you? Do you have a hard time imagining being completely open with your friend?

2. What would you like to change about yourself in this imagined situation?

Test Yourself

Based on how you are at work, at play, in your relationships, in your love attitudes, and at sex, rate your level of expression. By expression we mean generally how well you are able to convey what you think and feel to the people around you. Try to be very honest with yourself: remember this may be the first test you'll ever take that you can't fail.

EXPRESSION

	Work	Play	Relation-ships	Love	Sex
High					
Moderate					
Low					

The imagining exercise was about what you want to express, but this rating scale is about what you actually do. Look at the different ratings. We just want you to become aware that you might be using the personality skill of expression effectively in some areas of your life (a high rating) and not effectively in other areas of your life. Ask yourself about problems you might have in any of these five life areas. Do you have high or low expression skills in a problem area? It is probably becoming clearer to you that a problem area exists when personality skills are low. We don't want you to go ahead and try to solve your problem right now, we just want you to become aware. Consider thinking that a problem is really an area in which you have personality weaknesses.

Stretching Your Expressions

Read these sentences out loud three times. The first time in a very soft whisper, the next time in a normal talking voice, and finally in a loud voice. Find what volume matches your feeling about each sentence.

1. I am hungry.
2. I love you.
3. I am jealous.
4. Don't hurt me.

5. I'm glad to see you.
6. I want a raise.
7. I'm tired.
8. I am a good person. You're a good person.
9. I am tired of expressing less than I can.
10. I have what it takes.

Understanding your stretching exercise. These stretching exercises are preparing you for the real exercises. The ones in your life. You will begin to notice that many of the things you say don't match how you say them. You are quieter or louder than you want to be. You might find you don't pack as much power behind your words and voice as you want. Changing your expression by 10 percent can begin helping you have a new impact at work; more sensual expressions will affect your sex life. This simple stretching exercise is engaging your personality and your drive for fitness. Your outer self is moving toward your inner. A very natural psychological phenomenon is going to take place in your life. You are going to begin moving toward expressions which feel more like you. The movements may be small at first—but even the smallest ones will have large consequences.

These exercises can be practiced at home alone. If you want to become stronger at a faster rate, share these exercises with a friend. And talk about how you feel doing them.

This exercise will make you more aware of the way you normally express yourself. You will begin to realize that there are many times when *what you are saying* doesn't match *how you are feeling* when you are saying it.

Building Up Your Expression

It is important to keep strengthening your ability to express by trying out different things in public.

1. If someone at work does something you like, stop him and say, "I really liked that—I appreciate what you just did."

2. If someone does something you don't like or there is something you want changed, say so. Try "I don't like what you just said." (Do this only with people you know and trust, at first.)

3. Before you sit down to eat your lunch, say exactly what you want to eat and how you would like it to taste.

4. Clearly say *yes* five times today.

In Your Notebook

Now that you have tried building up your expression you probably have noticed something you have been vaguely aware of your entire life. There are social limitations on expression. Answer these questions:

1. List five social rules that limit expression. (For example—Don't be impolite. Don't say what you think. Be considerate of others.)

2. Cross out the rules that don't make sense to you.

3. Make your own list of five fitness rules that help you express yourself more. (For example—It's good for me to express how much I like someone.)

Instant Replay

Think about what you did today, and think about the psychological muscles you exercised. When did you get afraid? Did you worry? Were you awkward? Did you feel unnatural doing some of the things? Cap off your day by completing the following:

1. Write out ten things you would like to express. Use this form: "I would like to express _____." (For example: "I would like to express more happiness" or "I would like to express with more impact.")

2. What is your expression ideal? What would you be like if you could have complete expression skills? Talk to a friend about it, or write it out in your notebook.

3. What expression limits or weaknesses would you like to change, and how would you like to change them? Use this form for five of your weaknesses: "I would like to change my expression weakness of _____ by _____." (For example: I would like to change my expression weakness of quietness by talking louder.)

These expression exercises are designed to work in two ways. First of all, to stretch and stress your personality as you do them. For some people these will be big stresses and for others little stresses. Second, we are trying to show you how you can be. We hope you began to notice that many of the things that you would like to express you haven't been taught to express. The more you can understand the difference between what skills you lack and what you want, the easier it will be to take action. We also tried to make you aware of some of the social rules and limitations to expression —rules that aren't your rules. For some people it is hard to make up their own rules. But that is important.

The general **F-I-T**ness guides for expression are:

Feeling guide. When you are expressing yourself so that your inner self completely matches your outer self you will feel *satisfied*, even if the other person doesn't respond the way you want. Keep expressing until you feel that satisfaction.

Image guide. Use an image of yourself as a changeable, vibrant person, with many feelings about many things. Picture someone in motion.

Thought guide. Use the thought, "I am able to say whatever I feel, even if I don't know what I feel in advance." You don't have to preview your feelings and expressions; you can simply live them as they happen.

These general **F-I-T** guides can be used anytime, with anyone. But as you become more skilled at expression you will develop much more specific **F-I-T** guides for yourself.

WEEK ONE/DAY TWO: ACTIVITY EXERCISES

Now that you have been successful in jogging the expression side of your personality you are going to like today's program. You will be learning about activity. Your personality needs both to express and to be active. You can tell a person who is active by the way he moves. That's right. The *way* a person moves and not whether they move or not. When you move your arms, legs, and face you are using the dynamic of activity. When it becomes a conscious and natural part of your personality you will begin to really understand what a strength activity can be.

Warming Up

Activity, physical activity, requires space. Ask yourself how much space you require. Imagine you have a box around you that shows how much space you take up in a room. Is it a large box? A huge box? Or is it just bigger than your body? Imagine yourself entering a room with many other people in it. Do you take up a lot of space?

As children we tended to take up much more space than we do as adults. It seems strange but true—as we get larger we take up less space. We begin to feel uncomfortable moving our arms, talking, and moving. We become more and more passive as adults.

Understanding the activity warm-up. Most people are not comfortable with their bodies. They don't know how to use their arms and legs. They don't know what to do with their hands. They feel awkward. This means they are lacking activity skills. The warm-up exercise tries to help you recognize that you might not be taking up as much space as you could. Do you know someone who takes up a lot of space? The psychologically fit person does. He takes the space he needs. He has a presence. You can tell when a person has a presence because you are aware when he is in the room. Many people seem invisible.

Answer these questions about your own activity strengths and weaknesses in your notebook.

1. Is activity a personality strength for me?

2. What would I be like if I took up more space? How would my opinion of myself change? How would other people's opinion of me change?

3. What skills do I need to develop to be more active? (For example: I need to move my arms more when I talk.)

People sometimes want us to tell them what skills they need to develop. Part of the exercise is learning about what skills you need to learn.

This warm-up exercise is designed to help you notice the range and quality of your everyday movements. Many people never notice their movements. They live their lives in a little box. Their movements never violate the space of that little box. Your movements are a source of psychological strength. Begin noticing how you move. You have two arms, two legs, a face, shoulders—move them. You will feel better. You will develop a greater presence wherever you go.

People think that if everyone took up space there would be no room. The opposite is true. The more people in your life who take up space, the more your spaces overlap. You begin to live in a world with other people. You have the space to be yourself.

Test Yourself

Based on how you are in the five life areas we are testing, rate your level of activity or movement. By activity we mean generally how you move your body and how physically active you are in the ways in which you talk. Are you the one who goes up to touch and hug a friend? Do you initiate physical contact? Do you move around naturally and easily?

ACTIVITY

	Work	Play	Relation-ships	Love	Sex
High					
Moderate					
Low					

Stretching Your Activity Level

(To do alone.) Read these sentences aloud three times. The first time read with no movement at all, the next time with a moderate amount of movement, and the third time with vigorous movement. Find what movement matches each sentence for you.

1. I feel lousy.
2. It's no use.
3. I am not perfect and I'll never be.
4. I don't care if I'm not perfect.
5. I trust you.
6. You can depend on me.
7. I love you.
8. Let's go running.
9. I won. I won. I won.
10. I can do anything I want.

These exercises build personality power and presence. When you see a person who exudes power and presence, he seems to have an inner sense about his body. You also will begin naturally to move more—as you become aware of your movement potential.

These exercises can be practiced at home alone. If you want to become stronger at a faster rate, share these exercises with a friend and talk about how you feel doing them.

Understanding your stretching exercises. Did you notice any awkwardness during some of your movements? Keep in mind that awkwardness is the beginning of fitness. It takes strength to try and move in new ways.

Building Up Your Activity

(*Exercising in Public—When No One Else Knows You Are*)
Yesterday we worked on new ways of expressing in public. Now we want to increase your movement in public. This is a good way of positively stressing your personality.

1. When you are at work and you have something to say to someone else you work with, go up to him and put your hand on his shoulder.

2. When you are walking, be aware of moving and using your entire body.

3. When you meet someone you really like, go up and give him a big hug. Stand close to him and give him a second hug. Talk to him as you are hugging.

4. Whenever you are talking, try to remember what your hands and arms and legs are doing. Move your face more. Play with your mouth by opening it wider or smaller. Make your face come alive.

In Your Notebook

Think about all the social taboos there are against moving.

1. List some of the social rules that keep you from moving. (For example: Don't touch strangers. Don't be too physical.)
2. Cross out the rules that don't make sense to you.
3. Make up a list of your own fitness rules for movement. (For example: Movement releases tension. Activity stops my depression.)

Instant Replay

Get ready for bed. And then don't go to bed. Sit on your living room floor and *talk* about three new movements you made today (even if it is out loud to yourself). This breaks your old movement patterns.

1. In your notebook list ten ways "I'd like to be more active in my daily life by ——————."
2. Describe your ideal self in regard to movement.
3. How to change your movement weaknesses? Write five sentences: "I would like to change my movement weaknesses of —————— by ——————."

The general **F-I-T**ness guides for activity are:

Feeling guide. Every complete activity feels like a part of you, you will feel together, not scattered or fragmented. Use this feeling as a reference when you move.

Image guide. Picture your favorite graceful animal. Get the feeling of how it moves. Use that image-feeling to guide your own movement.

Thought guide. Use the thought, "I can always move. I'm ready." You don't have to know exactly how to move, just be ready for anything.

Use these general **F-I-T** guides until you develop your own special cues and guides.

WEEK ONE/DAY THREE: FEELING EXERCISES

When you feel bad, you sometimes might wish that you couldn't feel at all. Many people fantasize that if they didn't have feelings, their world would run right, and everything would be smooth. Psychologically fit people enjoy the feelings they have. Like spices, feelings make life different and intriguing.

Warming Up

Think about a time in your childhood, or a recent event, that made you very sad. As you think about it, allow yourself to experience a little of that sadness again. Allow it to spread over you like warm water. Close your eyes and remember growing up and hoping that everything would turn out. Feel your face and chin. Give in a little.

Understanding your warm-up exercise. In this exercise we are asking you to allow feelings that you already have to come to the surface. Most people want to control their feelings and keep them below the surface. People often think, "If only I could control my feelings, then. . . ." But this is wrong. The more you control—hold back—the less you know how to guide your feelings. The psychologically fit person doesn't try to control his feelings, instead he experiences them. The more that you get to know your feelings the closer your inner and outer selves come together.

In your notebook, answer these questions about your feeling skills:

1. How do I hold my feelings back? (For example: I deny I am feeling anything. I am afraid to offend someone. I get afraid to let down.)

2. List the feeling strengths you do have. (For example: I am sensitive to others' feelings. I feel loving. I am sympathetic.)

3. What would you have to learn to make your feeling
    skills stronger? (For example: I would have to learn to
    talk with more feeling. I would have to trust my feel-
    ings as much as I do my thoughts. I could learn to cry.)

These exercises are sometimes harder to do than the rest
because feelings come so much from the inside. There are not
many things you can do by yourself to deepen your feelings.
The best exercises we can give you involve two or more
people.

Test Yourself

Using the chart, rate your level of emotion or feeling in the
five basic life areas we are testing. Feeling is one of the major
keys to your personality dynamics. When you get back in
touch with your feelings then your personality will have more
emotional energy.

FEELING

	Work	Play	Relation-ships	Love	Sex
High					
Moderate					
Low					

It is surprising to find out that many problems exist because
people don't have enough emotional energy to change. They
have spent so much time controlling their emotions that their
inner life is completely out of touch with their outer self.

Notice in your graph in which area of your life you allow
yourself the most feeling. If you have problems in any of these
areas, could it be that you don't have enough emotional
energy?

Stretching Your Feeling Level

Read these sentences aloud three times—the first time in a
very dead voice, the second time in a normal voice, and the

third time with as much feeling as you can muster. The way to feeling more when you read these sentences is to recall an emotional incident while you are reading them.

1. I am feeling all the time.
2. I get afraid of showing what I feel.
3. I feel sad sometimes.
4. What I feel is important.
5. I want to feel myself and others around me.
6. I feel lonely and angry at different times.
7. I hate to see children treated badly.
8. I remember my childhood feelings.
9. I have the power to feel good.
10. I want to feel how strong I am.

Understanding this strengthening exercise. Most people are unaware of it, but we have feelings all the time. Sometimes they are big feelings, but mostly we have a certain level of feelings which tells us how to react to everything around us. This exercise is designed to help you contact your own feeling level. You might find yours is buried very deep and hard to find. If so, feeling is an area of weakness for you. For someone else, this simple exercise of feeling and remembering brings back a wave of feeling. Feeling is probably an area of strength for him.

This sentence exercise is similar to some of the techniques used in method acting, except that we are preparing you for your life experience rather than a performance. We are trying to kindle an awareness in you that you once had as a child. The more you become aware that you do feel, the more your feelings will naturally be integrated into your life.

Building Up Your Feelings

It is important to learn first to experience and feel your little emotions before trying to recapture your intense childhood feelings. The way to do this is to sharpen your awareness of what you are feeling.

1. When you are getting dressed for work, ask yourself how you feel. Are you looking forward to work? Are you happy to see anyone? Mad at anyone? Afraid of

anyone? Be aware of how you feel and your feelings of anticipation.

2. When you get to work, take five minutes and find the person you like the most and tell him. Don't discuss *what* made you like him, just that you feel good toward him.

3. As you eat lunch, look around at all the different people. Imagine yourself talking to them and asking them what they feel.

4. Think about how much feeling your parents expressed to you. There is a difference between knowing that they loved you and their showing you what they felt.

5. List the best feeling experiences that you ever had with your parents. Think about them.

6. List the emotional strengths and weaknesses you got from your parents.

7. Take time out and call your mother or father, and talk to them about how you felt as a child. Don't get into all the old stories and excuses, just say how you felt.

Answer these questions in your notebook:

1. What are your thoughts about feelings?
2. List the social rules that limit your feeling.
3. Cross out the rules that don't make sense to you.
4. Make up five new rules about feelings that would strengthen you.

Instant Replay

As you get in bed, think back about the entire day from an emotional point of view. Think about the times you felt something and didn't express it. What were the reasons you gave yourself?

Here is a good night exercise. Complete ten sentences that start with "I feel _____." Distinguish between your opinion about something and how you feel. Try to keep the sentences very personal.

1. What is your ideal feeling self like?

2. Complete five sentences with the following words: "I would like to be able to feel _____."

3. How would you like to be able to change your feeling weaknesses? Complete as many sentences like this as you want: "I would like to change my feeling weakness of _____ by _____."

The general **F-I-Tness** guides for feeling are:

Feeling guide. Real feelings move from inside to outside. You can feel centered inside yourself with every feeling as long as you identify it as coming from you and not caused by the environment. (E.g., "*I* feel angry," not "He made me angry.")

Image guide. Every different feeling has its own color and shape. Imagine your feelings as a constantly changing and fascinating color wheel.

Thought guide. Use the thought "I feel full" because feelings always fill you up; shutting off feelings leaves you with another feeling—emptiness.

Use these **F-I-T** guides for a time as you develop your own. Eventually you will have many feeling-, image-, and thought-guides that inform you about how to stay in touch with your feelings.

WEEK ONE/DAY FOUR: CLARITY EXERCISES

Clarity, for many people, is a made-up view of the world that substitutes for knowing what is really going on. Real clarity comes when your personality uses all its dynamics. It occurs when you combine your expression, your feelings, and your activity—with your understanding. When a very passive person thinks about relationships he might decide, "I don't have to declare and show my love—my wife knows I love her." Contrary to popular notions, clarity comes with action and personal experience. Clarity, then, is something that is functional. You can depend on it to help you become more psychologically fit.

Warming Up

We want you to do a very simple exercise: just identify ordinary things for what they are and are not. As you are getting dressed in the morning, and throughout the day, point to different objects and people and to yourself and say, for example:

> That's a coffee cup. It's not a house.
> I am me—I am not my mother.
> That is a dog—it isn't a tree.
> I am a human being—I am not a bulldozer.
> I am at work—I am not playing.

Repeat this exercise often throughout the day. You can do it silently, and you will be surprised by the results. You will begin to get very clear.

Understanding Your Warm-Up Exercise

Many people want to understand why the world exists, what the meaning of life is, and who they are. We don't pretend to have those answers, but what we do have in this exercise are the first steps toward an awareness of who you are and who you aren't. At times we combine things that don't really belong. How often have you said, "Everything is rotten, the world is terrible, how could people be that way"—when really you were saying something as simple as "I don't feel good"? Before you can understand the world you need to know yourself.

This warm-up exercise is to teach you to differentiate. Some people never know the difference between themselves and their parents. We are trying to make you aware of yourself as an individual. In that way you begin to have more of a present-day understanding rather than one determined by everything you have learned.

Everyone is aware, but it is often a negative awareness because you are more aware of what's wrong than what's right. Used to its fullest, awareness becomes an inner guide. This simple exercise will produce results that reveal what a keen understanding you do have—but are often too unskilled to put to use in your life.

In Your Notebook

1. What clarity strengths do you have? List at least five. (For example: "I clearly know when I am pretending." "I clearly see when other people are lying." "I know the difference between going for what I want and accepting less.")

2. What weaknesses in clarity do you have? (For example: "I am aware when a friend is not feeling good but I never do anything about it." That is a half awareness because you never know the real truth until you take action.)

3. What skills do you need to develop to make your clarity a greater strength? (For example: "I need to learn to say what I know"; "I need to stop looking for answers and living the solutions I already have.")

Test Yourself

We want you to rate yourself for clarity in just the same way you have done for the other dynamics.

CLARITY

	Work	Play	Relation-ships	Love	Sex
High					
Moderate					
Low					

In what area do you have the most clarity? Remember, we are talking about clarity in action. Do you have problems in one area that are related to your low level of clarity? Perhaps the most critical question to answer when looking at your graph is: Do you have an inner awareness which is not matched by an outer action? Clarity doesn't mean you have to lose emotional intensity or passion. In the fitness perspective clarity increases your ability to sustain good feeling. Real clarity will also help you to know when it is important to experience your feelings fully within yourself, or let them show to others.

Stretching Your Clarity

Write down five sentences about yourself that make complete sense to you (e.g., "I have brown hair"). Question every word in your sentences. Are they exactly what you mean? As you . go through the day, talk more clearly about yourself. Think about what would happen if you were completely clear about what was happening to you.

Sometimes a single word can make a big difference, e.g.,

"I feel sad."
"I feel very sad."

If you really feel "sad," not "very sad," telling yourself, "I feel very sad" will be confusing. Your inner self and outer self will move farther apart. Some people consistently over-play their feelings, and others consistently downplay theirs; neither feels good.

Compile twenty sentences, ten beginning with "I am clear about ———————" and ten beginning with "I am con-fused about ———————."

Understanding Your Stretching Exercises

These clarity exercises are some of the most demanding exer-cises you will ever do. Often people say things and act on them without ever questioning whether or not they make sense to them, or considering what consequences are in-volved. For example, someone might say when he is twenty— "America is a fascist country." That sounds good until you really question what he is saying. It might mean he is having trouble in school, or he can't find a job. But it probably also means he has never seen a fascist country. It might also mean he has a new insight into how things could be better and different.

Real clarity makes you a force to be reckoned with. You begin to hear, and to see, and to speak. This may seem too simple, but the psychologically fit person knows what they mean.

Building Up Your Clarity

Surprisingly, to exercise your clarity you sometimes have to do just the opposite. Make yourself as dumb as you possibly can. Try this exercise. Let yourself be in a fog about everything. Be careful not to do this for more than five minutes at a stretch. It can become addictive.

Now notice, while you are in the fog, how everything becomes very vague or very narrowed or very scattered. Different people become unclear in different ways. Become aware of how you do it.

In your notebook write the following:

1. What are your personal rules and limitations against being very clear? (E.g., "I'm not smart enough" or "I'm too young." Or "I have to be right.")
2. Cross out the rules that don't make sense to you.
3. Make up five new personal rules to strengthen your clarity. (E.g., "I can be aware of what's happening" and "I don't always have to be right.")

Instant Replay

When you get in bed tonight, be as smart about yourself as you possibly can. Try to see how your understanding has grown from a child's to an adult's. What were the personal strengths that you used to survive? Think about where you could have gone wrong. What were the consequences of living the way you did? How much potential do you really have?

1. Make up ten sentences that show what you want to be clear about: "I want to be clear about _____."
2. What is your ideal of clarity?
3. Write out five sentences that show your potential: "I would like to change my clarity weakness of _____ by _____." (For example: "I would like to change my clarity weakness of 'negativity' by admitting what is positive.")

The general **F-I-T**ness guides for clarity are:

Feeling guide. Clarity feels quick and sure rather than slow and hesitant. You can change and you can be wrong, but you always have some clear thought about what is happening to you. Don't wait for your thoughts to be complete paragraphs—a word or a sentence is a sufficient start for clarity, and you can always start.

Image guide. Clarity is bright, not dark. Imagine yourself as a light; sometimes you are just a penlight, sometimes you are a sun. You always have some light of self-awareness.

Thought guide. Don't demand that your thoughts about yourself be consistent, but do always have some helpful thought. Use this thought guide—"My thoughts can always tell me something."

You will never arrive at some Golden Rule of Clarity that always works. But you will develop a number of different **F-I-T** guides of your own that will add scope and brilliance to your personal clarity. In fact, developing **F-I-T** guides for yourself is a basic function of the clarity side of your personality.

WEEK ONE/DAY FIVE: CONTACT EXERCISES

Contact is the fifth personality dynamic—people are either moving toward or moving away from contact. The more that you move toward contact the better you feel. When you realize that contact is one of the keys to your personality and one of the keys to making yourself psychologically fit, you can maximize your personality. When you have real contact with someone, there is a sense of relief. No problem or thought or worry is too big or too overwhelming to think about.

Warming Up

Before you begin doing anything else, call up a friend and just talk. Don't spend time thinking what you are going to talk about. Do it now. When you talk, tell him or her you are doing it because you know how much you want contact.

Understanding the warm-up exercise. Contact is the only

personality dynamic you can't exercise by yourself. Become more familiar with your contact skills by answering the following questions:

1.   What are your contact strengths?

2.   What are your contact weaknesses?

3.   What contact skills do you need to develop a stronger contact dynamic in your personality?

Test Yourself

Rate yourself on contact as you have done for the other personality dynamics.

CONTACT

	Work	Play	Relation-ships	Love	Sex
High					
Moderate					
Low					

Many people think that it is impossible to make contact in work; it is possible only in play, relationships, love, and sex —but to varying degrees. What most people forget is how much contact they need and want so that they can feel good. Most people live their lives at a mediocre level of contact. They accept less than they want. They have accepted being alone and loneliness as a way of life. Loneliness is not the true condition of human beings. We need contact in every area of our life. Contact does not take away any of our passion or insight into life—it changes it from survival to pleasure. There are many philosophies and popular psychologies that promise you that if you gain control of yourself you will be able to resolve your life's difficulties. That isn't true. In the fitness perspective we stop pretending that we don't need contact. Everyone does. It is what makes human beings. It helps us reach our fullest potential.

Stretching Your Contact

Contact is one of the easiest personality characteristics to stretch and one of the quickest to lose its strength. Building your contact muscles is going to take a minimum of three days. Pick out someone you really like and set aside fifteen to thirty minutes each day to sit and talk with him or her. As you talk you will also use all the other psychological muscles that you are trying to build up. You can express, you can feel, you can be active, you can be clear. But give yourself fifteen minutes to talk only about yourself and to hear only about the other person. This exercise is one of the keys to psychological fitness. You can change your life by doing it. It makes you aware that you are alive and that you have a choice. Not an intellectual choice but a real life choice—of becoming psychologically fit.

DOs	DON'Ts
1. Do talk about how you feel.	1. Don't talk about the news.
2. Do try to express more feeling.	2. Don't talk about your belief systems (astrology, ESP, outer space).
3. Do try to be clear about what you are doing.	3. Don't talk about religion.
4. Do talk about how your life is now.	4. Don't talk about what to do.
5. Do talk about how you want your life to be.	5. Don't console each other.
6. Do talk about each other's strengths.	6. Don't point out what is wrong with each other.
7. Do talk about dying.	7. Don't talk in clichés.
8. Do talk about your choices.	8. Don't talk without feeling.
9. Do talk about your disappointments.	9. Don't analyze.
10. Do talk about your hopes.	10. Don't get psychological or psychoanalytic.

This exercise makes some people uneasy. You are going to find that you may be fairly superficial at first—getting down below your own superficial layer takes effort. Stick with it. The more that you do, the more you will experience and understand. Good luck—this is one of the big ones.

Building Up Contact

Wherever you go today make eye contact. If you go to the supermarket—take just a few extra seconds and make eye contact with the cashier. Try and make extra physical contact with friends. Be aware of all the ways that you and the people you meet avoid making contact. Use your fitness notebook to write down the observations you make.

1. What are the social rules and limitations against contact?

2. Cross out the rules that don't make sense to you.

3. Write out five new psychological fitness rules for contact.

Instant Replay

When you go to bed tonight, do not watch any TV or read or listen to the radio. Talk. If you are alone talk to someone on the phone. Talk about your fifteen-minute session. Work to integrate it. Talk about what you got from it and what you want to get from it. Talk about what you want to put into it tomorrow.

1. In your notebook write out ten ways you would like more contact: "I'd like to make more contact by _____."

2. What is your ideal of contact?

3. How would you like to be in regard to contact? "I would like to be able to change my contact weakness of _____ by _____."

Your **F-I-T**ness guides for contact are:

Feeling guide. Feel the impulses you have toward and away from people. Choose to move toward people instead of away. The way you feel as you choose is the key to contact.

Image guide. Picture yourself as a square cube and as a round ball. The cube is stationary, that is, nonchoosing. The ball moves. Contact is choosing movement between two or more people. It can make you "roll around" in a group of people. Every time you move toward contact, imagine the ball getting bigger and allowing you to make even more contact. But every time you move away from contact, imagine the cube getting bigger and becoming more stationary. It gets so heavy you can't move at all anymore.

Thought guide. People who slide away from contact often feel like they are being moved; they are not actively choosing. The thought you can use is "I can choose people." This thought makes you the active one—you do not have to wait to be chosen.

These general **F-I-T**ness guides can be used over and over again, but be sure to add your own as these start to lose their vitality for you. The main thing about guidelines is that they constantly need to be renewed and added to, or they lose their emotional charge. A good guide moves ahead of you and takes you into new territories.

RECAPPING WEEK ONE

You've begun. That's very important. Sometimes the hardest part of exercising is just getting started. Exercising parts of your personality is very much like exercising different muscle groups in your body. Week One is designed to give you more personality power. Your personality, when it is fully functioning, gives you the ability to make choices. When your personality is weak and not working, you are forced to make choices and decisions that you really don't want. As you exercise your personality you will find that you are beginning to have more choices. A choice to say what you think, a choice to express what you feel, a choice to be as active as you want, a choice to be as clear as you can be, and a choice to make more fulfilling contact. We want you to have the power to make these kinds of choices.

If you have done these exercises completely and continue the program, you will notice changes in your life. They will be subtle at first, but all the little steps you take will bring your inner and outer selves together. We are teaching you how to become the one you have always wanted to be. As you begin Week Two you will find you want to stop doing the exercises. When that happens it means you are becoming successful and getting closer to your own limitations on success. We have found with the thousands of people who have tried our fitness methods that the time they want to quit is not when they are having trouble but when they are becoming successful.

There are no social limits greater than your own limitations. A psychologically fit person faces the challenge of going beyond his own limits.

The main thing to learn from Week One is that you have strengths. We want you to remember those strengths and use them to help you become more fit.

The five basic personality skills are important keys to your psychological fitness. You might notice that what you think about as your inner self ("I am a feeling and sensitive person") just isn't the same as your outer self. Be aware of all those subtle differences. Throughout the next two weeks you will need to use the skills you have begun developing in Week One.

Give your natural drive for psychological fitness the chance to try out new behaviors in your life. It doesn't do any good just to understand psychological fitness—you are going to have to run the race to test yourself, break your limitations, and find your hidden potentials.

The way to use these exercises in the future is to keep the same format (warm-up, testing, stretching, building up, and replaying, plus F-I-T guides) but develop your own special exercises and applications. Thirty minutes a day of this kind of mind jogging four or five days a week will keep you in good psychological shape. If you ever get badly out of shape because you stop mind jogging for a period of weeks or months, just repeat the entire twenty-one-day program to get yourself back into the habit of psychological exercising.

Week Two: Building Up
to Peak Performances in Work, Play, Relationships, Love, and Sex

Now that you have begun to stretch your personality and build up new strengths, we want you to apply the new skills you learned to different life areas and achieve peak performances. You are moving from jogging to running; you are starting to go for distance and speed.

A peak performance does not mean "being the best." It means living *your* potential. When you live up to your potential in any area then you are giving a peak performance.

The exercises that follow will help you develop a new perspective which will keep you in shape psychologically. Long after you have finished reading this book you will be using the psychological fitness perspective to stay in shape.

You will benefit the most from this week's exercises if you read them in the morning before you start your day and answer the questions provided. We *want* you to take these exercises with you into your day. They will show you two things: first, how you now restrict your own psychological fitness in each of the life areas described and, second, how to expand so that you begin to attain levels of peak performance.

WEEK TWO/DAY EIGHT: HOW TO ACHIEVE PEAK FITNESS PERFORMANCES IN WORK

Before you can begin getting peak performances in your work you have to have a basic work fitness. The most important thing we can teach you about work is a new attitude. Many people believe that work is not real. Work is real. You will probably do some kind of work the rest of your life. Work is psychological energy in action. The more your energy is directed for your good, the more fit you will become.

If you are going to become fit at work, you have to get pleasure from it; you have to master it; you have to be self-motivated to do it; you have to be successful at it. When we talk about work fitness we aren't questioning whether you are a hard worker or not, or whether you are successful in your business or finances. Those are only a part of the goal to help you become *fit in work*. The usual story of the hard-working forty-five-year-old executive who drops dead from a heart attack is the story of a good hard worker but also the story of an unfit worker. Success in work must first be an internal success. You have to learn that liking to work and caring about what you do are the keys to work fitness.

You may not believe it possible that you can learn to love work. You can learn how to use this one-third of your day—completely. That means you use your potential to work 100 percent, and when you are finished you feel satisfied and are ready to do something else.

What Did You Score on Your Work Fitness Checkup?

WORK FITNESS	YES	NO
1. Do you enjoy work?	——	——
2. Are you financially successful, according to your own standards, in your work?	——	——

3. Are you successfully pursuing your chosen career? ___ ___

4. Are your work skills improving? ___ ___

5. Do you work well alone? ___ ___

6. Do you work well with others? ___ ___

7. Do you have a positive opinion of the way you work? ___ ___

8. Do you have a positive opinion of your potential to work? ___ ___

9. Have your attitudes about work improved, compared with earlier times in your life? ___ ___

10. Do you have the skills you need to work as successfully as you want to work? ___ ___

TOTALS ___ ___

If you had 8–10 yeses, you are a worker athlete. Your score means you have a strength in work. Now you need to become very conscious of this strength. The more you enjoy your work the more you put into it. The more you put into it the more satisfied and accomplished you will feel. But to completely enjoy work your inner self and your outer self have to agree. If your inner self wants to be a success at work and your outer self gives only three good days of work out of five, you have a basic disagreement. Make sure you use your different personality skills to stay in touch with how you feel on the inside so that your inner and outer selves work together. You have the potential to become a very fit worker. That means someone who gets pleasure and success simultaneously.

If you had 4–7 yeses, you are an amateur worker. This means you have the potential to be a worker athlete, but you don't put out. It also means that your inner self and your outer self are in disagreement over work. Either you are working in a way that doesn't feel good to your inner self or you are not working up to the potential of your inner self. In either case the disagreement causes you to be dissatisfied with your work situation. The basic difficulty that many people have with work is that it is not emotionally satisfying. They don't get what they want from it. Work, to be satisfying, has to become a place where you use your full potential. To do that you need to develop your personality strengths.

If you had 1–3 yeses, you are a worker spectator. It's time to do something about your work patterns and behavior. The more time you spend at this level of work the more the rest of your behavior will be affected. At this level your inner self and your outer self are out of touch with each other. What you are doing on the outside doesn't match what you think and feel on the inside. Everyone wants to succeed. When you don't take action toward that personal success, you are not living up to your inner feelings.

Key Question

Before we explain the key question for work fitness, we want to be sure you know that any question you answer no to in all of these surveys is a key question for you. Any no means you are lacking skills in that area. It immediately points out a weakness that must be developed for you. We have chosen just one question for each area because we have found that certain questions are basic to each. Whether you answered yes or no to the key question listed, read the answers carefully. These answers will give you important insight into any no answer you have given.

Do you enjoy work? If you want to develop your work fitness and have peak work performances, enjoyment is the key. If your work is unenjoyable you need to take new action. Set goals for yourself. Decide realistically how much money you want to make. Think about what position you need to achieve and what skills you need to acquire and develop to get what you want. Begin to match your real, inner feelings and the desires you have for yourself as a worker with your outside actions.

Next, *get the big picture.* Find out how your specific job relates to the big picture of your company. Once you know the big picture you know what makes your job important. Then start taking the time to get to know the people behind the other jobs. Remember the skills you practiced last week and start to use them more. Let people hear from you—make your presence felt. Get to know the secretaries and the bosses. The more you know the people behind the jobs the more power you will gain. But know them in a more personal and emotional way—don't just know their names or say hello to them as you walk by. Your work will become more enjoyable the more familiar you become with different people. You can't sustain psychological fitness with fellow workers—you have to develop worker friends, people you can actually talk to. Cultivate these relationships. Remember, activity is the key to work enjoyment.

Toward Work F-I-Tness

The general **F-I-T** guides for peak performance at work are:

Feeling guide. Everyone has had times in his life when he's succeeded 100 percent at something. Remember how good you felt when you were totally successful. Let the levels of feeling, clarity, expression, activity, and contact you had then help you change the way you are at work today.

Image guide. Think of the most successful person you know in your business. Imitate his or her most efficient work attitudes. Keep that picture in your head.

Thought guide. Keep the following thought with you at all times: "Am I satisfied with the way I'm working?" Answer it with your actions.

Use these guides a little more each day, each week, and each month so that you will start to satisfy your own work goals.

WEEK TWO/DAY NINE: HOW TO ACHIEVE PEAK FITNESS EXPERIENCES IN PLAY

To be psychologically fit you have to know when and how to play. That doesn't mean breaking Olympic records or sitting around playing checkers—it means a playful attitude. For some reason adulthood means seriousness. Serious work, serious sex, serious, serious, serious! Life is not just serious. It is playful. Play feels good.

Unfortunately, adult seriousness has become so strong in athletics that play for the sake of play is a hard thing to come by today. We are always trying to beat someone else or someone else's records.

In a recent report in *Psychology Today,* Jack Horn reviewed an article evaluating Little League programs in the United States. He found that while over 95 percent of the players said they just wanted to have fun and a whopping 75 percent said they'd rather play on a losing team than wait on the bench, the coaches thought they had to field the best team. The best team, it turned out, had a lot to do with parental urging. One-fourth of the kids and one-third of the coaches said they felt strong parental pressure.

HONESTY GETS MUGGED

An episode in Virginia Beach, Va., involving the manipulation of ten-to-twelve-year-old players in a Midget football league demonstrates once again that children's games are far too important to be entrusted to some adults.

Frederick Talbott, a staff writer for the Norfolk *Ledger-Star,* has brought to light proof that eleven of twenty-six members of one team—a team undefeated for two years —were too old (up to fifteen), too young, or did not live in Virginia Beach. The evidence surfaced when Mrs. J. A. Cox refused to go along with a coach who asked her to alter her son's age on his application blank. "We received five anonymous phone calls threatening our lives," Mrs. Cox said. One mother of a player in the league delivered a bunch of toughs to beat up the Cox boy; he ran inside and police were called.

"This is amazing," says Nick Sessoms, a City Parks and Recreation official who took part in an investigation by the city, "when you consider that we are talking about a game for children." The impact on children both on and off the team has been enormous. They have been exposed to a code that says cheating is defensible, and that lies are suitable when something as all-important as winning and losing is involved. Fletcher Bryant, the man who started the league in 1962, is irate: "This is the first exposure most of these kids have to organized sports."

An awards banquet was held for the offending team, the Courthouse Knights, at which everyone was assured that the Knights were still champs. Head Coach Frank Brunell said he had no idea there were eleven ineligibles on his team. Nevertheless, he and three other coaches have been permanently suspended from coaching city recreation teams in Virginia Beach.

No wonder our concept of play is jaded by the time we're adults! We need to remember that play is for pleasure.

While you may not be able to play a full two hours a day, you can have a playful attitude all day long. Being playful doesn't mean you can't be sad or you can't be thoughtful and understanding. But the overall attitude to life for the psychologically fit is one of playfulness. It makes work easier, and it makes living fun. It takes problems—even serious ones—out of the realm of the impossible.

If you ever visit a state mental hospital, one of the first things that you notice is how down and gloomy everyone is. If you run into a group of psychologically fit people, they convey the opposite impression—they are playful. Your playful attitude relates to your psychological fitness—it means you are no longer problem oriented. You are orienting toward your strengths, and that feels good. As you do what feels good you feel playful.

What Did You Score on Your Play Fitness Checkup?

PLAY FITNESS

	YES	NO
1. Do you enjoy playing sports?	___	___
2. Do you enjoy playing household games (cards, board games, etc.)?	___	___
3. Do you enjoy participating in competitive play?	___	___

4. Do you enjoy participating in noncompetitive play?   ___ ___

5. Do you play well with others?   ___ ___

6. Do you play three times or more a week?   ___ ___

7. Do you have a positive opinion of yourself as a player?   ___ ___

8. Do you have the skills you need to play as well as you want to play?   ___ ___

9. Do you play as much as you want?   ___ ___

10. Has your *satisfaction* with your play increased, compared with earlier times in your life?   ___ ___

TOTALS   ___ ___

If you had 8–10 yeses, you are a play athlete. This means your ability to play and be playful is a strength. You need to admit to this strength and begin using it to help develop weaker areas. The stronger you become in your ability to play the more resistant you become to psychological illness. You gain the play perspective. But a playful attitude must also be translated into taking specific time off from work to just play.

Take a close look at the questions you answered no to, and ask yourself how you can change these nos to yeses.

How can you use your strengths in play to improve your weaker areas? For example, did you answer yes to both questions 3 and 4? If you can only enjoy one kind of play, you are restricted in a part of your play behavior. If, however, you answered yes to both, ask yourself how you can use that playful competitiveness in work or in any other area you might need to develop. And if you are good at noncompetitive play, you can teach yourself how to have a better and more enjoyable sex life. Use your play strengths to develop a playful attitude. Your inner self and your outer self are close enough together that this area is a strength for you. Use it.

If you had 4–7 yeses, you are a weekend play athlete. You

are out of shape as far as play is concerned. This has serious consequences. It means you are weak in an area that gives perspective to many other areas in your life. Read these instructions carefully.

1. The first thing you need to do is take the time to play. You can never learn to play if you don't take the time. Nonplayers immediately say they don't have the time, they are too busy. If you don't *play,* your psychological fitness is being undermined. When you take the time to play you might be awkward at first. Set aside at least three specific times in your weekly schedule to play.

2. Remember how you played as a child. Remember how good it used to feel to really play long and hard. You had a relaxed, inner peace when you were finished. You weren't just not thinking or not working. Your whole body was tired and exercised. As adults, we often lose those body senses. Play requires that your body be involved. It is not enough to play Monopoly —you have to expand your play to include sports. Just as it is not enough to be a running nut—you have to learn to play quietly. Play is one of the only things that we do specifically to have fun. Once you have set aside time to play, find someone who is willing to play with you. Don't start off trying to be good. Start off playing. Whatever it is—play it, don't work at it. If you find that you really love some new game or sport, you have plenty of time to master it.

3. Find your play perspective. If you scored 4 or 5, your play perspective is very weak. You probably are one of the millions of people who say, "If I take a vacation all I want to do is get back to work." If that is you talking, surrender to your play time. It will make you a better worker, lover, and friend. Most of all it will make you feel better. Your inner and outer self are playing different games. The more you play, the more your entire life makes sense. You can play your way to fitness.

If you had 1–3 yeses, you are a play spectator. Your personality dynamics aren't working very well in your play area.

1. Look at your other life areas and find which one is your strongest. List three abilities that you have in that area. Then ask yourself how you can use those abilities to help you develop your weak play muscles.

2. Visit a home for the elderly or watch some old people at a park. Ask yourself if you are willing to become an old person in body and in spirit, or if you are going to be a playful old person. Face the consequences of your weakness in play. If you are not playing now, you are not going to learn miraculously how to play next year or the year after.

3. Make a list of all the possible games and sports you could play. Don't restrict yourself. Then choose one you are really interested in. Begin learning how to play that game or sport tomorrow. It doesn't matter *how* you begin—it just matters *that* you begin.

If your score fell in this range, a dangerous conflict is occurring. The disagreement between your inner self and outer self is actually aging you much faster than is safe. You are in trouble. This weakness is affecting your whole life, and you may not be aware of it. Take action now!

Key Question

Do you enjoy competitive play? Many people avoid competition, and others compete and don't enjoy it. Competition is good for your personality. But there is a certain quality that competition must have—it must be fun. The more fun in the competition the better it is for you. If you can enjoy the skills and strategy of your opponents, then you can discover what your strengths are and how you can develop your weaknesses into strengths.

If when you compete you find yourself hating your opponent and losing all sense of the game, then you are not enjoying yourself. Learn to play just for the sake of playing. Intense desire and concentration is good for your personality, especially if it occurs in a game setting. But if you lose perspective, if you feel as if you have to win or else, then you are no longer playing.

You can start competing at any game you play. The more you learn about it the more enjoyable it becomes. The more you play any sport the more you can appreciate the genius of the professionals who play it—from ballet to basketball.

Toward Play F-I-Tness

Here are the **F-I-T** guides for peak play performance.

Feeling guide. Concentrate on your *whole* body. Playing feels good all over. It is associated with all those pleasurable play sensations we used to feel as children. Express them and share them.

Image guide. Get the play perspective—the playful attitude. Some of the top professional athletes do their job, not just for the money, but because they enjoy playing. Read about them and learn about their attitudes.

Thought guide. This is easy. Think about having fun. All the time. Don't get lost in heavy, serious ponderings. *Think fun.*

Let these guidelines help you recapture some of the playful spirit of youth. We don't have to grow as old as fast as we think we do.

WEEK TWO/DAY TEN:
HOW TO ACHIEVE RELATIONSHIP FITNESS

We will concentrate on your relationships with your friends, but the same ideas are useful in all types of relationships. We are going to help you learn how to make your relationships work better, how you can learn to make more of them, and how to get the most out of them. One of the most important things to know about relationships is that everyone who lives and breathes needs them. Nobody can be totally alone and be psychologically fit. The five keys to fitness depend on interaction with other people.

First we will teach you about relating to people in general and to friends. Then we will move to relationships with a lover. And finally in the last section we will explore your sexual relating. In all of these sections we are exploring your psychological attitudes and how you can strengthen them.

The key word in relationships is not the noun—relation—but the verb—relating. When we relate we build relationships. We get feedback, we get the yeses and the nos; we get the praise and the blame. Without relationships our personalities would become very flabby and stale. In relationships we test out our ideas, we get our physical and emotional needs satisfied, we verify our humanness.

What we have found is that most people don't use their relationships to their maximum. They only use them in spurts. Throughout the exercises we want to teach you how to use your relationships so that your entire personality finds ways of stressing itself and growing stronger.

What Did You Score on Your Relationship Fitness Checkup?

RELATIONSHIP FITNESS

		YES	NO
1.	Do you enjoy your friendships?	——	——
2.	Do you trust and depend on your friends when you need someone to lean on?	——	——
3.	Do your friends trust and depend on you when they need someone to lean on?	——	——
4.	Do you see friends regularly (at least three times a week)?	——	——
5.	Do you have close friends of both sexes?	——	——
6.	Do you have long-term friendships of three years or more?	——	——
7.	Do you have a positive opinion of your ability to make and keep friends?	——	——
8.	Do other people have a positive opinion of your ability to make and keep friends?	——	——
9.	Are you satisfied with your friendships?	——	——
10.	Do you have the skills you need to make and keep as many friends as you want?	——	——
	TOTALS	——	——

If you had 8–10 yeses, you are a relationship athlete. That means you have developed the strengths necessary to build, keep, and use relationships. One of the most important things to do with your relationships is to continue to use them. Since you are strong already, all you need are a few exercises to stress your personality and tone yourself in this life area.

1. Sit down with a friend and tell him or her four inner fears about yourself. As you tell them, also be aware of what strength it takes to do it.

2. At another time sit down with a friend and tell him or her four things you would like changed. When you do this, *do not* be negative. It is best to do it with the same friend that you did the first exercise with. Be supportive.

3. The third exercise actually takes an entire month to complete. Make an agreement with a friend to share with each other a living diary, every day. For ten minutes or more, talk to each other at the end of the day and share what you felt and thought during the day.

You can use your strength of relating in other areas of your life. Whatever other area you are weak in you can begin to strengthen by relating to someone who is strong in that area so they can teach you how to improve. Then you are using your strength to overcome a weakness.

This high score means your inner self knows the possibilities in a good relationship. Keep working on this strength of yours. If you continue to develop it, it will change your entire life. It requires that you use all your strengths, and this gives you a better inner sense of who you are. The more we show ourselves to other people, the more we let ourselves be known and the more we know ourselves.

If you had 4–7 yeses, you are a weekend athlete in relationships. This often means your relationships are fine only if everything is going right. The biggest things missing are consistency, depth, and persistence. To become more psychologically fit you have to be consistent with your friends and those around you. You need to be dependable and reliable. You develop depth and stretch the limits of your ability to express by talking more with more feeling and clarity. If you have a hard time expressing yourself, use your friendships to help you learn to talk more. Ask a friend directly—"Teach me how to talk in new ways."

Finally, you need to develop persistence. If a friend is feeling bad, don't leave him or just give him some clichéd advice. Help him work the problem out. In the same way, if a friend is feeling good, help him celebrate it.

You will find that when you relate consistently, deeply, and persistently there are going to be times when you feel awkward and don't know what to do. Those are the very moments when you are developing your psychological muscles and endurance. It means you have gone further than ever before. That is the way toward greater psychological fitness.

We don't have to give you any particular exercises for this level of relationships because you have enough relationships and must deal with them often. But you are missing some of your opportunities to develop these relationships.

The lack of agreement between your inner self and outer self puts you in conflict. You move toward, then away from, relating. That often means the inner you knows what you want, but the outer you doesn't know how to do what the inner self wants. You need to develop your relating skills. Remember to use each chance you get to increase these skills.

If you had 1–3 yeses, you have the potential to develop a new area in your life. You are a *relationship spectator.* Your fitness in this area is probably very low. If you allow yourself to develop this area it will have a profound effect on how you feel about yourself. A person who has friends is not lonely. He has someone to lessen his disappointments, someone to help him face the world, someone to celebrate with.

The very first thing you can do is to pick the one person in your life you like the most. It could be your mother, father, brother, sister, mailman, next-door neighbor. The only requirement is that it be someone you like. Once you find that person, you need to realize that relationships are *built*, not discovered. Here is how to start building your relationship with the person of your choice:

1. Ask this person to tell you all the good things about himself.

2. Have a conversation about your childhoods. Don't reminisce—ask each other questions about beliefs, and values, and patterns of behavior from your pasts.

3. Make a point to talk every day in a new way to this person. The more time that you spend with him the more your relationship will build. As you feel more comfortable allow yourself the pleasure of revealing little worries and fears, little hopes and desires that you might ordinarily keep secret. If you are persistent and honest you will soon find that you have a friend.

There are few life areas that are more critical for your over-all fitness than relationships. Your low scores indicate that your inner self, your outer self, and your skills of connecting them are out of order. Let your inner self start to reach out.

Make this a first order of importance for yourself. Your ability to withstand crises and keep your identity is seriously undermined by this weakness.

Key Question

Are you satisfied with your friendships? Many people we have talked with have friendships, but they allow themselves the attitude of the unfit—"Well, it's better than nothing." Often that is not the case. Being alone can often give more insight and add more depth of experience than a mediocre friendship. A real friendship must have depth and quality. A satisfying friendship is one that meets your needs as a friend. If you are living with unsatisfying relationships, you are not using your personality strengths to get what you want. A friendship is a place to explore your weaknesses and to hone your strengths. That's what a friend is for—someone you can be yourself with, someone you can change with.

Many people relate to no one except those people whom they intimately know and care about. They are cheating themselves out of the experience of meeting different people at different levels. Relationships do not all have to be soul-baring experiences. You can have a relationship with the man at the hardware store. Don't just go buy something you need, buy it from someone. When you frequent a restaurant get to know the owner. Introduce yourself. Tell him what you like about his restaurant. People want to hear from other people. It is a great feeling to go into a store and be recognized. You can make the biggest city in the world a place filled with lots of different kinds of relationships. The more you relate the better you will feel. It is up to you.

Toward Relationship F-I-Tness

Read these **F-I-T** guides for relationship fitness.

Feeling guide. The main feeling you get from a relationship is one of solid contact. If you feel that there is a mutual consistency and reliability between you and some number of special friends, then you have the contact that is required in a good relationship.

Image guide. A building without a foundation would tilt, bend, and soon break apart. So will your relationships if you don't keep building good foundations. Imagine a big, well-supported building—that's what you want.

Thought guide. Think this: "I need friends—people around me to help me as I help them." Remember there are no psychologically fit hermits.

Build your relationships with these guides. Try them today and use them over and over whenever you can.

WEEK TWO/DAY ELEVEN: HOW TO ACHIEVE LOVE FITNESS

We have found that as people become more psychologically fit they become more loving. First they begin to love themselves. The person who doesn't love himself is harsh and cruel to himself and to those around him. If you can be hard on yourself, eventually you will use those same negative skills on those around you.

Once a person loves himself, he naturally and easily begins loving others. As you become psychologically fit, that feeling of love will begin to grow in you and eventually spread to others. You will notice how love makes everything easier. You give yourself more of a chance, you give those around you more room to be themselves, you enjoy others more, and you help them change without criticizing them. The more that you learn to love, the more people are drawn to you and the more benefits of love you will reap. You will have more power and influence because people will trust you more, and feel that you will not abuse their trust.

As your general ability to love grows, so does your ability to love one person. You will find that you can give yourself in love to one person in new and deeper ways and learn what it means to find love, stay in love, and love being in love.

Being in love with a single person and having a loving attitude reaches into every area of your life. Your entire personality changes. You work better, you have better sex, you play better, you relate better because you are learning from love to both give to yourself and give yourself.

What Did You Score on the Love Fitness Survey?

LOVE FITNESS	YES	NO
1. Do you enjoy making physical contact with your lover?	——	——
2. Are you good friends with your lover?	——	——
3. Do you share your secret thoughts with your lover?	——	——
4. Do you share your intimate feelings with your lover?	——	——
5. Have you ever had a long-term love relationship (three years or more)?	——	——
6. Do you have a positive opinion of your ability to love?	——	——
7. Do other people have a positive opinion of your ability to love?	——	——
8. Are you satisfied with your love relationship?	——	——
9. Do you have the interpersonal skills you need to have a love relationship?	——	——

10.   Do you have a positive opinion of your potential to love?   —— ——

                         TOTALS   —— ——

If you had 8–10 yeses, you are a lover. We would call you an expert in love.

1.   Ask yourself if you are using your personality dynamics of expression, feeling, activity, clarity, and contact to their fullest. In order to do this you have to admit that you do love. In admitting this you have to give in to the feeling and learn to hold on to it. Even when you fight with your lover—which can be good for you—don't allow the fight to take away your awareness of your love.

2.   A positive fight is good for stretching your personality and making it firmer. Have a positive shouting match with your lover. Yell how much you love each other, shout about all the good things you notice and like about each other.

3.   Spread your ability to love to other areas of your life, especially your weakest life area. Instead of talking about your weaknesses, love your potential for strength. Talk with your lover about a weak area that you want to develop.

Love gives a person depth and quality. Allow your love to change you. Love—when you seek and want it—is a new state of consciousness and reality. Use it, for love must grow.

If you had 4–7 yeses, you have the opportunity to change the tone and feeling of the rest of your life. You are having bursts of love awareness, but you aren't giving in to them completely. You are a *weekend lover.* You exercise your ability to love but not often enough to establish a one-to-one relationship that changes both of you.

1.   Sit with your lover and spend ten minutes each day saying everything that you want. You can start with material things and then move to more personal wants and needs.

2. Admit every day that you want to be in love. Talk about your lover to people you know. Tell friends about your lover. Talk about your love, and you will learn about love.

3. Once a day ask your lover to do one thing for you and then do one thing your lover wants you to do.

4. If you are very serious about learning to love, then spend one hour every night with your lover in bed. Turn off the TV and just talk and touch and visit. Share your hour consciously. To stay in love you have to keep building. Then your love becomes the foundation of your life.

Love needs to be lived. If you sit on the fence too long you will get stuck there. Learning to love means learning the psychological, emotional, and interpersonal skills of love. Your inner self says "go," but your outer self says "how?" You have to admit what you want most and seek the skills you need.

If you had 1–3 yeses, you are a love spectator. You could have someone in your life in a way that you might have only fantasized about.

1. Make a list of all the things that you want from a love relationship: "I want _____."

2. Ask yourself how strong you really are in the area of relationships in general. Do your relationships start to grow and then stop? How do you usually stop a relationship? Make a list of the excuses you use to stop love relationships.

3. Start building a love relationship right now. The person that you like the most and think you might love is the one to start with. Love doesn't mean sex in this case.

4. Find a person whose love and relationship skills you respect. Visit with him once a week and let him teach you about his skills. Sometimes it is easiest to develop your own skills by imitating someone else.

You are at a critical stage. Love gives us a sense of ourselves, of goodness, of being connected in our lives. Your inner self is confused by your outer actions. You are suffering from a serious lack of skills. Clearly admit to yourself every day that "I want love."

When most people think about love relationships they imagine some magical state called "being in love" that people fall in and out of. You can fall in love with a special person —someone whom you especially give yourself to—but one person is not enough. The magic land of love needs lots of room to grow. If you love only one person your love will become the target of all that is good and bad in your life. Love needs other love to support it. Men need to love other men. And women need to love other women. And men need to love women. And women need to love men. Adults need to love children. And children need to love other adults besides their parents. Bonds develop between people who can give and receive love. It is really a deepening of a friendship. When a person is loved and loves, then his or her special love is strengthened and grows.

Love is all the actions you take and all the movements you make to show your love. Like the tree that it is, as it grows it changes the landscape of your personality.

Key Question

Are you satisfied with your love relationship? If you answered no to this question, you are not using your personality dynamics to help your love grow. Love is actually time shared with a person who is sharing back. To share positively you have to be psychologically fit. Otherwise you will share your unfitness. As your personality becomes fit you will find you have a limitless love that you can share your entire life.

Many people forget love can be a verb. It is full of action. Love gives us the contact we need to lead a full and satisfying life. We are all naturally in love. Be what you are—in love with the life that you have.

Toward Love F-I-Tness

Today's **F-I-T** guides for love fitness are:

Feeling guide. The best feeling guide for love is depth. Love
    is a very deep friendship, so deep that everything the

person you love does affects you immediately. Be aware of these levels of effect in your love relationships.

Image guide. Think of two friends you know or two lovers you know who love each other very much. Visualize how they are physically, and hear how they talk. Plant this picture in your head as a reminder.

Thought guide. "Love needs to be lived and experienced" can be a guiding thought for all your love relationships. Make your actions reflect this thought whenever you're with someone you love.

WEEK TWO/DAY TWELVE:
HOW TO ACHIEVE
PEAK SEXUAL PERFORMANCE

Before we teach people any specific sexual skills we help them to learn about their feelings. Not just their sexual feelings but all of their feelings. When people become intimate with their own feelings, then they are able to experience acts of intimacy. Sex is an act of emotional intimacy, first, and an act of the body, second. If you are not comfortable with your feelings, then you will not be able to experience your full sexual potential.

Most people believe that sex is what takes place between two people who are engaged in some sort of genital activity. If that were true then we would only be part-time sexual beings—computers with genitals. When people fail to understand the breadth of their sexual nature they have difficulty developing their sexuality.

Sexual development is as necessary as intellectual development, physical development, and moral development. When you are not functioning as a sexually developed person all other areas of your life are distorted. Sexual fitness makes it easier for you to carry on a long-term emotional life partnership with someone you love. Fitness enables you to keep your desire intense. Fitness allows you to deepen your ability to be honest and vulnerable.

The main key to sexual fitness is desire. The single most confusing aspect about sex is that our desires wax and wane almost by themselves. If your desire is intense you see only with love's eyes, and everything is exciting; but when desire is on the wane you often turn cold and bitter toward the person you once loved.

If your sexual feeling doesn't allow you to maintain your sexuality during intercourse and throughout your whole relationship with a person, you are experiencing a sexual problem.

A man is not impotent alone. He is impotent with a woman. A woman is not frigid alone. She is frigid with a man. Since sex involves two people, then sexual fitness must necessarily be between two people.

It may seem strange in the era of the sexual revolution that we propose a model for sexual fitness that includes fidelity, loyalty, love, truth, respect, monogamy, and intimacy—but we do.

Sexual problems do not just happen. They are developed. The ability to have satisfying sex is a great psychological strength. When you experience any sexual problem you are experiencing an undeveloped personality strength. Ideally, as we encountered undeveloped areas of our life and personality we would simply try to develop new skills. Instead, when faced with a weakness, we often conclude that we have a problem. In no other area are people more apt to conclude they have a problem than in their sexual functioning.

What Did You Score on Your Sexual Fitness Checkup?

SEXUAL FITNESS

		YES	NO
1.	Do you enjoy sex?	——	——
2.	Do you have sex as often as you want?	——	——
3.	Do you usually express your secret thoughts during sex?	——	——
4.	Do you usually express your intimate feelings during sex?	——	——

5. Do you have the sexual skills to do what
    you want to do during sex?   ___   ___

6. Do you have sex regularly (at least three
    times a week)?   ___   ___

7. Do you have a positive opinion of your
    sexual life?   ___   ___

8. Do other people have a positive opinion
    of your sexual life?   ___   ___

9. Have your attitudes about sex improved,
    compared with earlier times in your life?   ___   ___

10. Are you satisfied with all aspects of your
    sex life?   ___   ___

                              TOTALS   ___   ___

*If you had 8–10 yeses, you are a sexual hero or heroine;
you have sexual strengths.* You need to expand these strengths.
Take your ability to have a single sexual relationship and begin developing your sexuality. That includes your entire attitude toward life and other people. You can begin getting more
pleasure from your work, more pleasure from your play, more
pleasure from your friends. That does not mean you become
a sybarite, but a person who gets pleasure and satisfaction
from what he or she does. Begin to use some of your sexual
strengths to develop any weak areas.

1. For any questions that you answered no to on the
    checkup, list four ways you can begin answering yes to
    them.

2. How would you change if you had all yeses? What
    personality dynamics would you have to strengthen to
    achieve this?

3. When you are with your lover, on five different nights,
    exaggerate each one of the personality dynamics (ex-
    pression, activity, feeling, clarity, and contact)—one to
    a night. You can do all sorts of exaggerated love ex-
    pressions and many different kinds of exaggerated

movements; you can exaggerate your clarity and your feeling; finally, exaggerate the amount of contact you make. This exercise is entertaining as well as deepening. You will find that as you make greater contact the more you play with the dynamics.

4.   The next time you have sex with your lover, don't do anything. Get done. Let your sex partner just do to you. After you are satisfied, reverse roles.

Your high scores indicate how close your inner self and outer self are in sex. This area can be a profound way to change your entire life. The more you give yourself openly and honestly to your sexual life, the better you can feel. If you answered no to any questions, develop the skills you need to change the nos to yeses.

Sex is only for pleasure—there is no outside standard. Make your sex life as full as it needs to be to satisfy your inner self.

If you had 4–7 yeses, you are a weekend lover. There are many questions that you are answering no that could be yeses. Think about becoming a total lover—giving your heart completely to the one you are in love with.

1.   Vulnerable—if you haven't ever thought about vulnerability as a strength, do. Spend some time each day— just a few minutes—being vulnerable. Say vulnerable things and do vulnerable actions with your lover.

2.   Strength—you must begin relying on your love. Use it as a strength and use it every day. Become a love addict. Call your lover. Write your lover letters. Give in totally to developing your love strengths.

3.   Sharing—spend a week doing nothing but concentrating on the person that you love. Find out all about his or her childhood, favorite things, strengths, and weaknesses.

4.   Spend the weekend in bed. Get rid of the kids, if you have them. Store up on your favorite foods and treats, and spend the entire weekend in bed. At least once an hour kiss for five minutes and tell each other why you love each other.

You need to follow the exercises because your weaknesses in this area can turn into problems. If your sexual life isn't completely satisfying, other dissatisfactions can begin to appear. Work or play cannot replace sex. The stronger you become in this area the more secure your identity will become.

If you had 1–3 yeses, you are a sexual spectator. You are missing out on one of the most profound and important aspects of your own psychological fitness. You scored low on love and that means you have the potential to develop an entirely new area of your life. When you develop this area you will begin maturing emotionally. You will see and hear things not objectively, but through the eyes and ears of love.

1. Sit down for ten minutes and try and tell yourself why you can't ever love anyone in the way that we are talking about.

2. At another time say out loud all the reasons why you really do want to love someone and someone to love you.

3. If you don't have a lover, your next step is to find one. Remember, a lover starts out as simply as someone to date, to hold hands with. Begin building a relationship in the ways you learned about yesterday.

4. GIVING IN—to learn to love you have to develop the strength of giving in. Whenever you can, give in to your lover.

5. Learn how to hold hands. Spend time just holding hands wherever you are.

6. Start kissing. Give your lover 200 kisses a day.

7. When you have sex, ask your partner what feels good and what feels better. Be aggressive. When you are ready, do the exercises in the higher scoring areas.

You need to question the sexual beliefs you have grown up with. Make a list of them in your notebook. Your low scores indicate that you may only know what not to do—instead of how to do what you want. Begin asking people you trust about sex. Use your outer self's action to educate your inner self to what is possible. The lack of congruence between your inner self and outer self means you have never learned how to be sexually fit.

Key Question

Are you satisfied with all aspects of your sex life? Many people like some parts of their sex life but are afraid to ask for everything that they want and afraid to do everything they want. They begin holding back and hoping that their sex lives will get better. More often than not, they become resigned to an incomplete sex life. They forget that sex gives them the opportunity to exercise all the dynamics of their personalities (expression—saying what they want, activity—doing what they want, clarity—knowing what they want, feeling—experiencing what they want, and contact—making a bridge to another person).

Sex is not a once-monthly experience. Frequent sex allows you to have all kinds of sexual intensity. Sometimes it can be mellow sex, just a way of talking with your sex partner, and at other times it can be exciting sex. But it should always be satisfying, based on the way your body feels. Learn to use sex to help yourself feel better.

Toward Sexual F-I-Tness

The **F-I-T** guides for sexual fitness are:

Feeling guide. Rather than concentrating on only sexual feelings, be aware of your body's general sensuality. Know that you have an alive, adult, and sexually responsive body.

Image guide. Sexual fitness is based on choice and action. Picture yourself making active choices about sex rather than waiting passively for something good to happen.

Thought guide. The primary thought to keep in mind is "My body is alive." Listen to its aliveness, and use it to help you make sexual choices and take sexual actions.

These guides will put you on the road to sexual fitness.

A RECAP OF THE SECOND WEEK

This week you have begun to apply some of your personality strengths to important areas of your life. You have learned the key questions to ask about these life areas so you can achieve peak performances. Use the weekend to focus on the life area you most want to develop. Be sure to update your fitness notebook.

Here's a sample from one person's notebook—just so you can get an idea of what you might notice and do.

JULY 30, SUNDAY

Had trouble doing sex exercise. Couldn't stop putting myself down. Don't feel like a hero at all—more like a dead duck. Noticed that I say about half or less of what I think and then I get bored. Can't get used to saying thoughts and feeling during sex or before. I do start to feel more desire when I talk, but then the feeling shifts over to nervousness when I don't talk.

To talk or not to talk. That is the sexual question for me. The sexy answer is to talk and the turned-off answer is not to talk.

I'll try again on my date tonight. I'm going to remember the sexy answer as much as I can. I'll even ask my date to help me keep talking—even if I just yak about my own interests!

An additional bonus of the psychological fitness program is that if you scored low in one area, you can do the exercises for your particular score, and, later on, you can do the exercises for the higher scores. This means that you have enough exercises to help yourself become exceptionally fit for a long time.

Week Three: Peak Emotional, Intellectual, Physical, Moral, and Sleep and Dream Performances

During these five days of exercises we are going to help you learn how to get peak performances from your emotional life, intellectual life, physical life, moral life, and your sleep and dreams. Don't forget that a peak performance does not mean you have done better than other people. It doesn't even mean you have achieved your own best-ever performance. A peak performance occurs when you are using all of your skills and potentials at one time. That moment of 100 percent effort is the moment of peak performance. It feels good to you and it brings together your inner self and your outer self. It is the experience of psychological fitness.

WEEK THREE/DAY FIFTEEN:
HOW TO ACHIEVE
PEAK EMOTIONAL PERFORMANCES

You will attain a peak emotional performance when you can answer yes to all ten questions in the checkup. Every time you answer no it means you have more potential than you are using and have the chance to have an even fuller life.

What Did You Score on Your Emotional Checkup?

EMOTIONAL FITNESS	YES	NO
1. Can you express anger easily?	——	——
2. Can you express sadness easily?	——	——
3. Can you express happiness easily?	——	——
4. Can you express fear easily?	——	——
5. Do you express your emotions to others easily and freely?	——	——
6. Do you use your emotions to help you to make your decisions?	——	——
7. Do you have a positive opinion of your potential to be emotional?	——	——
8. Do you have a positive opinion of the way you are using your present emotional skills?	——	——
9. Are those around you as emotional as you want?	——	——
10. Do you have the skills you need to be as emotional as you want to be?	——	——
TOTALS	——	——

If you had 8–10 yeses, you are an emotional athlete. This means that your inner self and your outer self are matched. What you feel is in harmony with how you act. You need to begin using your emotional strengths as a way of naturally stressing your personality. Learn to keep yourself fit and growing emotionally by stressing your own personality through exercise.

If you had 4–7 yeses, you are an emotional weekender.
Your inner self and your outer self are having some real disagreements. You have the impulses and the ideas of how you want to be emotionally, but you don't use all of your personality dynamics. Your expression is likely to be weaker than your clarity. Use your clarity to develop your ability to express your emotions. Start by admitting out loud what you know about yourself. Then you won't be in conflict. Many of your problems in this area come from not giving in to the emotional potential that you have.

If you had 1–3 yeses, you are an emotional spectator. You are out of shape emotionally. Your inner self and your outer self have forgotten each other, and you need to get them back together. The same energy you are spending holding in your emotions could be used to make you feel better and live a more effective life.

It is pretty obvious when someone is physically unfit, with a pot belly, but someone unfit emotionally is much harder to detect. The latest advances in psychology and medicine show that a strictly clinical view of illness is not sufficient for good medical care. Rather, there is a move to holistic medicine and the consideration of the emotions of patients along with their physical ills.

Key Question

Take a look at the answers you gave to each key question carefully. The answers and advice we give for each of them provide important insights into all the other questions on the surveys.

Do you express your emotions to others easily and freely?
This is one of the key questions of the emotional fitness checkup. If you can't express your emotions then your emotions are out of control. Emotions are very paradoxical. The more that you try to control them, the more out of control they get. And the more you learn to express and use them, the more in control you are. Expressing your emotions gives you a way of strengthening your personality. It gives you a way of finding out how much staying power and clarity you have. If you express and run away, you are showing a lack of emotional skills. But if you can express and stay and express more and

allow your emotions to change, then you have found a key to emotional fitness.

Anger is a good example. Held-in anger turns against you by producing tension. But when it is healthily expressed, it can change your life. You can practice your anger skills with a good friend. Decide on a topic to fight about for five minutes, and have an enjoyable exchange of emotional opinions. Be positive. Each shows the other how to stand ground when necessary. Then enjoy your anger. Use it to get closer and to blow up obstacles to being close, rather than to blow up in anger.

Sadness is the gentle sister of anger. You can practice feeling sad by watching sad movies or reading sad books and letting yourself cry rather than locking the emotion inside. Get the help of your anger partner with this, too. Write each other sad little stories or poems. Sadness can teach you how to love. It helps you become more human.

Most people think that when it comes to happiness, they are pretty fit. But we have seen too many people who require a drink or drugs to loosen up. And too often the feeling of happiness is not sustained. These are weaknesses. Happiness is an active feeling. If you have trouble finding and keeping it, then you need to take some psychological action. Make a list in your notebook of things, and people, and places that make you happy. Ask other people what makes them happy and how they learned to be happy. Happiness is a way of action. You can learn how to be happy more of the time.

The way you handle fear is also a sign of your psychological fitness. Most people are afraid of fear. But fear is a terrific personality strength. Animals know and use fear to keep from getting hurt. When we know and use our fear strengths, then we keep ourselves out of dangerous situations. The less we know about our fears, the more they tend to stop our actions. But as we recognize the positive sides of our fears more, we can begin to use them. Make a list of your ten strongest fears. Talk about them—become familiar with them. Fear is an instinctual heritage that can keep you emotionally and physically out of danger.

Most people fear their emotions because they have been taught that their feelings are destructive and embarrassing.

What you feel is wonderful. When you hold in and get out of touch with what you feel, your feelings become nightmares. They turn into psychosomatic eruptions, they turn into distress, they turn into problems.

Toward Emotional F-I-Tness

Your **F-I-T** guide for your emotional life is very important.

Feeling guide. Your main emotional feeling guide is a sense of contact. Are you contacting people around you with your emotions? Make as many emotional bridges as you can.

Image guide. Imagine yourself in the middle of a group of people, some of whom you know and others you don't. Picture yourself walking through the crowd slowly with your arms stretched out. Every time you touch someone with your arms, make an emotional bridge to them— express some feeling. You are like a mass of energy causing little sparks whenever you come in contact with someone else.

Thought guide. Think Italian. A common thought/image association with Italians is their lively style of talking. Think of yourself as an Italian exaggerating your expressions with gestures and body movements. Have fun with it.

Remember, your emotional side has a powerful influence over the rest of your life. Use the **F-I-T** guides to develop your emotional fitness.

WEEK THREE/DAY SIXTEEN: HOW TO ACHIEVE PEAK INTELLECTUAL PERFORMANCE

You do not need a high I.Q. to begin having peak intellectual performances. Intellectual performance depends on your using what you have.

There is probably no psychological strength that is more overworked than the intellectual. Sometimes what we think seems more real to us than what we feel. We get convinced that we can think our way out of problems which need other psychological skills. The intellect is only a part of our overall makeup.

If people used all their psychological strengths, the intellect wouldn't have to work so hard. Because the intellect often has to hold the personality together all by itself, it comes under stress attack. For example the intellect is overstressed when a person believes that his view of the world must be the right one. He isn't aware of what else is possible. That process is both protective and defective. It protects the personality when no other strengths are around to help it out. But it is defective when the intellect tells the person that he can't do something or he should avoid something he doesn't need to.

The intellect, when used in harmony with all the other life areas, becomes a major strength that is delightful.

We want you to take a new view of the intellect. Think about it as a tool. Does this tool work well for you? What other tools does it work with? How can you put this tool to better use?

What Did You Score on Your Intellectual Checkup?

INTELLECTUAL FITNESS

		YES	NO
1.	Do you *enjoy* thinking and solving problems?	___	___
2.	Are your intellectual skills improving?	___	___
3.	Do you share your ideas and thoughts with others?	___	___
4.	Do you learn easily?	___	___
5.	Do you have the skills you need to be as intellectual as you want to be?	___	___
6.	Do you think creatively?	___	___
7.	Do you have a positive opinion of the way you use your present intellectual skills?	___	___

8. Do other people have a positive opinion
    of your intellectual abilities?   ____ ____

9. Do you have a positive opinion of your
    potential to be intellectual?   ____ ____

10. Are you satisfied with your intellectual
    abilities?   ____ ____

                                          TOTALS   ____ ____

If you had 8–10 yeses, you are an intellectual athlete. That
means your inner self and your outer self are in harmony. You
are using your intellect rather than getting used by it. The
more that you allow yourself to use this strength to keep developing your other personality skills the fewer arbitrary
meanings you will ascribe to things and the more you will
enlarge your understanding of how things are.

This score also indicates that you tend to use your intellectual strengths creatively. You have an ability to break down
your intellectual boundaries by using your creativity. This
can be a great source of pleasure for you because it makes you
keep growing intellectually. The best sign of creative thinking
is how much pleasure it gives you.

If you had 4–7 yeses, you are a weekend intellectual. You
may be very intelligent, but you are not getting a peak performance from your intellectual strengths. Many people con-
fuse peak performance with understanding things. Your intellectual strength is only a part of your overall makeup. The
questions in the checkup are designed to see if your intellect is
integrated into your life. You have definite weaknesses in this
area. Your inner self and your outer self are in disagreement.

You need to begin to integrate your intellectual strengths
into the rest of your life. Start to put your ideas and thoughts
into words. The more that you share what you think and the
less you try to prove what you think, the stronger you will
become. You can start this out by talking with someone about
a specific intellectual weakness you have. Focus on it. Talk
it out. Hash it around and have fun with it. Now you have expression, contact, clarity, and activity all coming into play to

increase your intellectual performance. This allows your skills to develop in more than one area at the same time.

If you had 1–3 yeses, you are an intellectual spectator. If you are very smart that means you are watching yourself. Your inner self is out of touch with your outer self. You don't have the skills to make the connection between the two and begin getting a peak performance from your intellectual strengths.

But don't turn on yourself intellectually just because you have never learned the skills you need to bring your potential out. Begin to learn new intellectual skills. Find someone who scores higher on their intellectual score than you—someone whose skills are more refined. Let them teach you more about your strengths and weaknesses.

The more you allow others to teach you what they understand, the more you will learn. You are learning not only what they are thinking, but how to focus, how to understand.

A good sign of improving intellectual skills is your ability to focus on what you are doing. Allow yourself to be taught more about your strengths and weaknesses by learning how to focus on them. The intellectual skill of focusing helps you do anything for longer periods of time and with greater understanding and pleasure. It becomes a way of learning and developing your intellectual abilities. Once you have these basic intellectual skills, you can learn anything.

Key Question

Do you have the skills you need to be as intellectual as you want to be? This question takes a lot of emotional and intellectual honesty to answer. If you answer no to it, then you are face to face with a cause of many of your problems. If you don't use your strengths fully, then you begin to feel unfit. Your self-image is lower than it could be. In some ways you have a safety valve—you think, well, if I ever did use it, then things would be different. Having potential is a strength, but having the skill to use that potential is an even more effective strength. There is a good exercise you can use to help yourself get face to face with your beliefs about how good you could be. Write in your notebook, or think about, the following sentence: "I could ——————— if I ——————."

The more that you come to understand what you think your potential is, the closer you are to your inner self. The next step is to develop the skills that bring your inner self and your outer actions together. It's time you got tired of thinking about who you could be rather than being who you are.

Toward Intellectual F-I-Tness

The **F-I-T** guide for intellectual fitness concisely summarizes the advice we have given your intellect so far.

Feeling guide. Whether or not you are good at solving problems, you should enjoy the use of your intellect. If you work on a problem's solution so much that you forget how you feel, you aren't getting a peak intellectual performance. If you can always keep an emotional perspective when solving problems, you will think clearer and feel better.

Image guide. Aristotle. Plato. Greek philosophers. These are your images—men who were great thinkers, but whose prime concern was man's humanity.

Thought guide. Here is a good thought exercise to guide the development of your thinking abilities. Write in your notebook ten sentences you can think of beginning with "I can easily solve ———." Be aware of what you are saying about yourself as you do this. Pay attention to your strengths.

These guides can help you become, intellectually, the person you've imagined but kept hidden.

WEEK THREE/DAY SEVENTEEN: HOW TO ACHIEVE PEAK PHYSICAL FITNESS PERFORMANCES

A potential source of pleasure, physical fitness often becomes a source of shoulds. "I should be exercising more but. . . . I should do my running but. . . . I should do my stretching but. . . . I should lose weight but. . . ." Such shoulds can do more damage than being out of shape. So there is no reason for you to beat your brains out for not running, swimming, skiing, etc. Your physical fitness, if it is to be effective, needs to become first and foremost a source of pleasure for you.

One of the most important things to realize about physical fitness is that it is only a part of being in good shape overall. The more that you come to see that each area we are teaching you about is only part of a whole, the more you can put it in perspective. If you have a particular strength in any area and you enjoy expanding and using it—do it. If physical fitness is a great strong point for you, then use that strength to help you with weaker areas. If physical fitness is a weak area for you, take the time to begin learning the skills you need to develop this potential pleasure.

If you are not psychologically fit you can't become physically fit. Fitness is more than a healthy heart and well-conditoned lungs—it is an attitude: "I am changing my life through my actions. I have the choice." If you are running to get rid of emotional tension, you will never finish the race. Your psychological nature is so complex that you must pay close attention to each life area, or a neglected potential will pop up in some other place in your life as a problem.

We want you to become more aware of your body and your movements. We hope you will develop an attitude of wanting to do the exercises you need to do to stay fit. As your fitness attitude develops, you'll find you are using it in all aspects of your life.

What Did You Score on Your Physical Fitness Checkup?

PHYSICAL FITNESS

		YES	NO
1.	Is your physical fitness improving?	—	—
2.	Are you fit and trim? A good weight for your age and health?	—	—
3.	Do you have physical vitality, an energetic, healthy presence?	—	—
4.	Are you physically flexible and supple?	—	—

5.   Do you have a positive opinion of your potential to be physically fit?   ___ ___

6.   Do others have a good opinion of your physical fitness?   ___ ___

7.   Are you well coordinated?   ___ ___

8.   Are you satisfied with the way you are using your present fitness skills?   ___ ___

9.   Have your physical fitness attitudes improved, compared to earlier times?   ___ ___

10. Do you have the skills you need to be as fit as you want to be?   ___ ___

TOTALS   ___ ___

If you had 8–10 yeses, you have the attitude of an athlete. Take a serious look at your no answers and find what you need to do in order to change those into yeses.

1.   AWARENESS. Stay aware of your body all the time. Try to learn to think from your body, talk from your body, feel from your body. Your body will guide and protect you. You will find that you become much more emotionally stable as you allow yourself to use your body as a guide.

2.   FEELING. If you run or exercise, be aware of the feeling in your body. Work to make your body become more alive. Don't use your physical exercises to control your body. Make sure that the exercises you do are giving you more feeling. Often when people become totally engrossed in physical fitness their bodies become increasingly immune to feeling. Then they mistakenly think they are feeling better.

3.   LIFETIME. Exercise is a lifetime activity. Work on the pace and the level that always gives you more and more enjoyment, rather than a distant, exterior goal. Let your body choose the goal. Don't try to become some fantasy

marathon runner. Run or exercise for the enjoyment of it.

If you had 4–7 yeses, you are a weekend athlete. You aren't serious and you are headed for serious trouble. No matter how successful you may be in whatever you are doing, you'll remain psychologically unfit because you are physically unfit.

Becoming physically fit allows you to take care of the very root of your life—your body. Your body must be sound and functioning at its best if you are going to live your entire lifetime. Try these ideas:

1. GET NAKED. That's right, get naked in front of your own mirror and take a good look at yourself. How do you look? Do you like the way you look? List all the parts of your body that you like and the parts you don't like. Take the actions outlined in the next three steps to begin to rearrange your body so that you are totally satisfied with it.

2. MOVEMENT. The first necessity of physical fitness is movement. You don't need a running suit or sweat pants, or a coach. Start moving more. Walk around the house or apartment more. Exaggerate your movements. Help yourself become a movement addict. Consciously move more than you normally would at least five times a day.

3. ACTION. Buy yourself a good physical fitness book and get started. But make this action a part of your overall new psychological action. Be aware of what you are doing—know that you are choosing to act and to continue acting.

4. SATISFACTION. Learn to satisfy yourself with your exercises. Find the exercises or the sports that are just right for you, ones that fit your personality.

If you had 1–3 yeses, you are a physical fitness spectator. You can begin by standing up right now. Shake your legs and arms. Raise your voice. You have a lot of inertia that can all be turned into kinetic energy.

1. COMMITMENT. Some of your commitment time and energy is spent on the wrong things. You have prob-

ably tried to become fit often enough but you invari-
ably failed. Make a list of all the things that you are
committed to that keep you from following through
with your physical fitness.

2.   PARTNER. Find a partner. It is only the rare bird who is
      willing to suffer the pangs of becoming fit all by him-
      self.

3.   SCHEDULE. You and your partner set a schedule for
      yourselves for exercise and weight. Work it out care-
      fully so you can stick to it. Then, at exercise time, don't
      let anything interfere with your activity. Make it the
      most important thing you are doing. Tailor the schedule
      to yourself. The program should be perfect for you.

4.   CONTRACT. This is the kicker. You've probably tried to
      exercise before, but found it just too hard to keep it up.
      Well, now there are two of you; make a contract with
      each other. If either one misses a single day or session,
      he has to deposit a certain amount of money in a joint
      savings account. When you have finally reached your
      goals, use this money to take a play vacation, go
      skiing, visit a tennis ranch, stay at a good country club
      for a weekend, or go swimming or surfing. This way
      both of you work to get both of you fit.

Key Question

*Are you satisfied with the way you are using your present
fitness skills?* Often when people decide to get fit, they try to
buy fitness by collecting sweat suits, jump ropes, stop watches.
It's better to begin using the skills you already have. Take
stock of your fitness attitude. Begin living a more fit everyday
life before you start running three miles a day. You can gain a
fitness awareness that allows you to keep moving and be
active at all times. That awareness will change your attitude
about many things. It will help you tone up your life. Fitness
is a lifestyle rather than a style of exercising.

Once you've integrated fitness into your life, start to keep
a physical fitness diary in your notebook and also on your calendar. At the beginning of each month record your weight,

pulse, and your general feeling level. This constant checkup will allow you to keep track of yourself. Improving is difficult if you have a concrete idea of what you'd like to be. But it becomes easy when it is just you reaching for your potential.

Toward Physical F-I-Tness

Your **F-I-T** guides for physical fitness are:

Feeling guide. Learn to always become aware of a new part of your body. Exercise so that you are always developing some undeveloped areas, not to build muscle, but just to become fit.

Image guide. More important than being in shape is whether or not you are getting in shape. Imagine your body as a finely machined tool that you have for your whole life and that you must keep in good shape if you are to benefit from it. Develop the long-term fitness mentality.

Thought guide. *Think* physical fitness. Express your goals by saying, "I am going to be. . . ." When you begin to know that you have the potential to be fit, you have acquired the most important skills you will ever need.

Be aware of the condition of your body now and use the **F-I-T** guides to think about how you want your body to be and what you will do to get it that way.

WEEK THREE/DAY EIGHTEEN: HOW TO ACHIEVE PEAK MORAL PERFORMANCES

Moral and ethical behavior is an important part of psychological fitness. When an individual's personality is out of balance he does things which are out of balance. When a person is feeling good and functioning at a high level of psychological efficiency, he or she acts more ethically and morally. The person's behavior springs from an inner consistency rather than a religious or spiritual attitude.

What Did You Score on Your Moral Checkup?

MORAL FITNESS

		YES	NO
1.	Are you trustworthy?	——	——
2.	Do you take responsibility for your actions?	——	——
3.	Are you more moral and ethical than at earlier times in your life?	——	——
4.	Are you honest?	——	——
5.	Are you fair and just?	——	——
6.	Do you respect the moral values of others?	——	——
7.	Is your moral code flexible?	——	——
8.	Do you have a positive opinion of your moral and ethical beliefs and behavior?	——	——
9.	Do other people have a positive opinion of your moral and ethical beliefs and behavior?	——	——
10.	Are you satisfied with your own moral and ethical behavior?	——	——
	TOTALS	——	——

If you had 8–10 yeses, you are a moral athlete. Moreover, your moral and ethical fitness is a by-product of your behavior rather than something you have to consciously think about first.

1. Write out your moral and ethical beliefs. Make them very specific. It should not be a long list.

2. Do you hold these beliefs now, or are they just holdovers from your past? Have you ever challenged these value systems—have you ever asked questions about their usefulness and validity? If not, begin to do so.

If you had 4–7 yeses, you are a weekend moralist. You are in conflict more than you are aware.

1. Make a list of all the moral and ethical qualities that you would like to possess.

2. Ask yourself how lacking these values interferes with other areas of your psychological fitness (friends, lover, work, etc.).

3. Begin talking about a new value system for yourself based on how you feel. Think about developing a value system that could change as you change, but not just to suit your convenience.

If you had 1–3 yeses, you are a moral spectator. Your moral and ethical fitness is very low. You are not using your sense of what is right to maximize your own psychological fitness.

1. Make a list of your parents' value systems.

2. Think about what is right with each of their values and what is wrong with each value. What are the limitations and what are the qualities of each value?

3. Cross out the values you no longer believe in.

4. Imagine yourself as a person without any value system. Fantasize a world where you could do anything that you wanted and get anything that you wanted. Really expand on the fantasy. Ask yourself how you would feel.

5. Now repeat the fantasy, but this time imagine yourself as a successful person with a very suitable moral and ethical code of behavior. Which one feels better?

6. Create a moral code and standard for ethical behavior that would help you to feel better, live better, and be more successful. Base it totally on your own experience. Then talk to friends and read them what you have written. Ask them what they think about it.

7. Make a contract with yourself. Each day try to live by the code that you have created. See how you feel. Be persistent.

The ideal of a personal code of ethical behavior frightens many people. They want to live by external rules—Presbyterian, Catholic, Jewish, Islamic—not recognizing that values considered as rules limit your growth. Meaningful values can be better seen as guides rather than restrictions. The biggest reason most people don't want to create and live by their own moral codes is that then they *become responsible* and can be held accountable to themselves and to those around them. If you break someone else's rules, it's not so important. But when the rule is your own, then you can't ignore it. It is with you at all times.

When you are moral you become more consistent. People can depend on and trust you and respect you. All your other behavior gains a moral and ethical slant. You become an example rather than someone who follows examples.

Key Question

Do you take responsibility for your actions? This single question is perhaps one of the most difficult in the entire chapter. Taking responsibility means that you know you are doing something because you have chosen to do it. You can be responsible only as much as you are aware. The more you are aware the more responsibility you naturally assume. Make a list of all the different things in your life that you want to be responsible for, then make another list of the things that you don't want to be responsible for. As you become aware of what you want and don't want to be responsible for, then you can choose.

Toward Moral F-I-Tness

The following guides will help you develop your sense of moral fitness in your behaviors:

Feeling guide. No matter what happens, you should feel good enough about what you've done so that you can stand behind it. This doesn't mean you should be inflexible. It means that your actions are guided by emotional honesty.

Image guide. Many images come to mind as guides, from religious leaders to Abraham Lincoln. But the most important image for morality is yourself. Do you act the way you want others to see you? Make the inner goodness and honesty that you were born with be the image you live by.

Thought guide. Ask the following question of yourself for each behavior you display: "Does what I'm doing now feel *right* to me?"

Nurture your value system. It is a precious and valuable commodity.

WEEK THREE/DAY NINETEEN: HOW TO ACHIEVE PEAK PERFORMANCES IN SLEEP AND DREAMS

A peak performance in sleep means being able to fall asleep quickly and to sleep soundly and restfully. And when you awaken from sleep you should feel rested and ready to go. When your dreams are not peak dreams then you wake up in the morning less able to start the day from your psychological strengths. When dreams are passive, symbolic, when the dreamer is victimized, when there are strangers in dreams, and when there is anxiety and apprehension, it is a sign of unfit dream behavior. We have been working with dreams for over ten years and have shown that it is possible to dream dreams in which you are active, you feel good, you have friends, there is little or no symbolism, and you wake up feeling good. This type of dreaming lets you have break-through or peak dreams.

What is important is that your peak sleep and dream behavior become an overall skill and not a periodic experience. You should become able to sleep and dream in such a way that you gain from your nighttime experiences. When your inner self and your outer self are matched, then you have the potential to have peak sleep and dream experiences. But when you experience a separation and disconnection between the two, your dreams become troubled and your sleep is often disturbed. It has been reported that over 60 percent of the population reports having some sort of trouble sleeping at some time.

We think that a person's psychological fitness is reflected in his dreams. It means that the way you behave in the day is very similar to your behavior in your dreams, and vice versa.

We have called that the *parallelism hypothesis*.

Dreams test your success in doing fitness exercises. The more fit you become the more you should notice your dreams changing. You will know when you are doing your exercises right when your dreams begin to change. You should notice the change immediately. When people's waking lives change, then their dream life changes.

Your dreams reflect the process of learning as well as the process of solving your problems. During your dreams you are practicing the skills of thinking in new ways that you can carry over into your waking life. The more your dream and sleep behavior becomes fit the more you will have completed the full cycle of psychological fitness—from waking to sleep and from sleep to waking. You become the chooser, the doer, the guide, and the follower of your fitness behavior.

What Did You Score on Your Sleep and Dream Checkup?

SLEEP AND DREAM FITNESS

		YES	NO
1.	Do you use your dreams to help yourself understand and change your life?	——	——
2.	Do you have the skills you need to understand and use your dreams?	——	——
3.	Are you satisfied with your dream life?	——	——
4.	Generally, do you feel good in your dreams?	——	——
5.	Do you remember your dreams three times a week?	——	——
6.	Do you discuss your dreams with friends and acquaintances at least once a week?	——	——
7.	Do you feel rested and alert upon waking?	——	——
8.	Do you sleep soundly?	——	——
9.	Do you fall asleep easily and naturally without drugs or alcohol?	——	——

10. Are you satisfied with your sleep fitness? —— ——

TOTALS —— ——

If you had 8–10 yeses, you are a dream athlete. You can begin making a few exercise adjustments, and you will have a consistent peak performance from your sleep and dreams. Your score suggests that your inner self and your outer self are getting closer together. The more you allow yourself to take action in waking the more you will take action in your dreams. It is important that you get the cycle of psychological fitness going (from waking to dreams to waking). Here are some exercises you can do to begin exercising your dream personality.

1. Start taking a look at your dream personality. How active, how expressive, how feelingful, how clear, how much contact is there in your dreams? If you are low in any of these categories you need some more work. Notice that how you are in your dreams is often how you are in waking.

2. Take your dreams seriously. Remember you are the *dream maker.* Listen to what you are telling yourself about yourself.

3. Start your own dream group. Once a week meet with your family or friends and exchange dreams.

If you had 4–7 yeses, you are a dream amateur. This means that your inner self and your outer self are far enough apart that the only way they make contact with each other is through symbols in your dreams. You need to begin facing the symbolic nature of the communication between your inner and outer self. At night your inner self is taking over and telling you how well your personality is really functioning. Here are some dream DOs and DON'Ts.

DON'T:

1. Don't try to interpret your dreams. Don't look for sexual or psychological meaning behind every symbol.

2. Don't try to control your dreams by programming them before you go to bed at night.

3. Don't keep a written dream diary, yet. Later you can record your most important dreams, once you know how to use them.

4. Don't use the dream books which tell you 40,000 dreams and their meanings.

DO:

1. In the morning when you wake up and want to remember your dreams, ask yourself, "How do I feel?" Dreams are pictures of feelings, and you need to get in touch with the feelings first; the pictures will come naturally when you remember the feeling.

2. If you can't remember a dream, make one up based on the feeling you awakened with. Just make a simple dream, with pictures and dialogue.

3. Do talk every day with another person about your dream, and about how you felt when you awoke.

4. Do make sure that you have a good and consistent sleep schedule. Make sure your body gets the rest it needs. Research has shown that we need seven to eight hours per night on the average. However, everyone has his own patterns and specific needs. Become aware of what sleep schedule feels best to you and stick to it.

If you had 1–3 yeses, you are a dream spectator. A large part of your life is beyond your reach. Your inner self and outer self are doing battle during the night. It's time you brought some light and understanding into your sleep and dream life.

Remembering your dreams is a first step. Set your clock for one half hour earlier than you normally wake up. As soon as you get up, be aware of how you feel. Start writing down whatever you are feeling and thinking, even sentence fragments.

Your low score indicates that your waking personality is not functioning up to its potential. You need to concentrate more on it while looking to your sleep and dreams to verify the results of what you are doing.

We are going to teach you the twenty-five most important sentences you have ever read. Think of five important things that you do and every day write out five sentences following each of these five different formats in your dream diary:

> I would like to be more active when. . . .
> I would like to be more expressive when. . . .
> I would like to feel more when. . . .
> I would like to have more clarity when. . . .
> I would like to make more contact when. . . .

These are what we call remembering exercises. The more that you do them the more you remember that you have an inner self. When you remember your inner self, you will begin remembering your dreams and will become aware of how your dream personality is functioning.

Once you remember your dreams you can follow this simple exercise to help you work with your dreams.

> If I were more active in this dream then. . . .
> If I were more expressive in this dream then. . . .
> If I felt more in this dream then. . . .
> If I were clearer in this dream then. . . .
> If I made more contact in this dream then. . . .

If you ask yourself those five simple questions for each dream you remember, you will begin exercising your dream personality. It will get stronger and your next checkup score should improve dramatically.

Key Question

Generally, do you feel good in your dreams? This question is of critical importance. It reflects the harmony or lack of it between your inner self and your outer self. There obviously are no monsters chasing you in the real world. The conflicts that you perceive in your dreams are the conflicts between your inner self and your outer self. The more that the conflicts are faced and worked out the more satisfying and enlightening your dreams will become. A conflict in your dreams means you have the potential for more peace. Don't be frightened by disturbing dreams. Use them as indicators for yourself of how much potential energy you have. You need to learn the skills necessary to turn that potential into kinetic energy. Your dreams are a powerhouse.

This question also tells us about the quality of your sleep. Dreams that leave you feeling good are relaxing. This relaxed state makes your sleep more restful. But when your dreams are negative, your body gets upset also. A parallel activity occurs when you're sick. Your body's ills are translated into your dreams. Sleeping soundly and feeling rested indicates that you are relaxing at night. This relaxing allows you to have more pleasurable sleep.

Toward Sleep and Dream F-I-Tness

The **F-I-T** guides for sleep and dream fitness are used during the day.

Feeling guide. Your goal is to feel rested and peaceful, especially in the morning when you wake up and at night before you go to sleep.

Image guide. Talk about your dreams. Discussing your dreams gives you the chance to begin exercising your waking personality as well as bringing your dreams out of the dark. The more you talk about your dreams the more you will understand what you are trying to say to yourself each night.

Thought guide. Think this: "How would I like my dreams to change?" Talk about different ways you want to be in your dreams. Make these wants and changes conscious during the day by sharing your ideas.

You *can* change your night life. Don't be its victim. Start to actively interfere with your sleep and dream habits.

A Recap of the Third Week

Use the weekend to review this week's work. Go over the more difficult exercises and modify them so that they become easier for you. Also use these last two days to see how each day has built on the one before. You should now have a clearer picture of your strengths, weaknesses, and skills. You are gaining the ability to use your personality dynamics and bring your inner self and your outer self together.

We recommend that you continue to use the skills we have taught you to develop a personal, on-going fitness program. Remember, fitness is a lifetime activity.

You now know from experience that psychological fitness is the *process* of becoming more fit in work, play, friendships, love, sex. Your emotions, your intellect, your body, your values, and your sleep and dreams change, and the process is controlled by the five personality dynamics: expression, feeling, activity, awareness, and contact.

Know your personality strengths and use them to develop new strengths from the weaknesses. Apply your strengths to areas of your life to achieve peak performances. Enjoy your fitness through continued exercise and growth.

PART 3

How to Change
Problems
into Strengths

A New Way to Look
at Your Problems

Many people believe that to achieve their peak potential, they must become great at something. They have to have some single outstanding quality that makes people pay attention to them. They are wrong. If you learn to make your life happen, you will find your fullest potential. Everyone has a chance to fulfill his own potential in life. That is why psychological fitness is so exciting.

In the chapters that follow we are going to discuss many of the common problems that people have. Our goal is to teach you to look at psychological problems from the fitness perspective.

THE FITNESS PERSPECTIVE

Every problem that you have is actually an attempt at a solution. For example, alcoholics don't drink to become alcoholics.

They begin drinking because it is a short-term solution to a problem. They feel bad before they start drinking, and they begin to feel better as they drink. Only they now have another problem—drinking.

What happens when a person gets drunk? Research studies on the brain physiology of alcohol show that alcohol mainly affects the inhibiting centers of the cortex. Intoxicated people experience a release of their feelings (technically, alcohol effectively removes the cortical control of the limbic system). Unfortunately this way of releasing feelings also decreases clarity and motor control which leads to accidents and crimes.

The person who drinks is indirectly trying to 1) increase his feeling, 2) increase his expressiveness, and 3) increase his contact.[1] He has taken an action with disastrous results.

But his problem is not the drinking. It is inside, and like so many other people with problems, his inner and outer selves are at war. His inner self has feelings and needs that the outer self doesn't know how to fulfill. The outside problems just reflect these interior conflicts.

WHY PROBLEMS ARE CREATED

Many people begin to think they are their problems. They begin to identify themselves as a problem: "I am a shy person," or "I am depressed," or "I am fat." We are never just our problems. If we were, we wouldn't know we had one. We would think that fat, depression, or shyness was our natural state. Our problems arise when we don't have the skills we need to bridge a gap between our inner self and outer self. A problem means that our outer self is not functioning well and our inner self knows it. People have problems because they don't have the skills to bring their inner selves and outer selves together. People fill the gap between their inner and outer selves with problems. The greater the distance the more room for problems.

[1] You can also understand why Alcoholics Anonymous is an effective method for many alcoholics. AA demands that alcoholics make contact with other members and express how they feel.

The real solution is to bring the inner and outer selves together. In our lives we will always have thoughts and behaviors that are troublesome, but they only become problems when our inner self and outer self are far apart. When our inner and outer selves are closer together, then troubles are just troubles.

In the chapters that follow we will discuss how problems work—frustration will change to frustrating, shyness will change to withholding, worries will change to worrying. We will turn your static problems into processes. It is much easier to strengthen and change a process than it is to solve a problem. Often, for each static problem you solve, ten more appear. But when you learn the processes at work behind your problems, solutions will develop and multiply.

HOW PROBLEMS ARE CREATED

People create personal problems because they don't have the skills to keep the outer self functioning well. The basic personality skills we have discussed earlier—expression, activity, feeling, clarity, and contact—are what determine how well our outer self functions. If you don't have these basic skills, it's hard to keep your outer self functioning at a high level, and it is equally hard to bring your inner and outer selves together.

Understand this one basic idea and you will give yourself a head start in changing your problems into strengths. *Every common psychological problem contains a hidden strength; you do not need to develop the strength—you already have it.*

This means that every problem has certain highly developed personality skills associated with it—and at the same time other highly underdeveloped personality skills. For example, a chronic worrier has certainly developed the ability to feel, but he has overlooked the development of the personality dynamic of clarity to help him differentiate what is a real feeling and concern and what isn't. He hasn't developed activity so that he can learn to do something about his feelings.

When you have incompletely developed skills, it is impossible to function well because your inner and outer selves are not in harmony. In the psychological fitness approach you can discover the hidden and misused personality skill or strength and begin using it in a new way. The strength was developed during all the years you created the problem. Think about it. Your problems, like worrying and blaming, you've already practiced for years. It is easy to understand how, with so much practice, you developed a lot of skill.

The trick is to use your skill in a new way, a way that will uncover the hidden strength beneath the problem. Then you will be able to let the skill work for you rather than against you.

GENERAL MISCONCEPTIONS ABOUT CHANGE AND PROBLEMS

In the chapters to come we will discuss many of the specific misconceptions people have about phobias, frustration, worrying, and other problems. But there are three misconceptions that are widely held about psychological problems in general.

Healthy people don't have psychological problems. This is untrue. The fact is: It is normal and natural to have psychological problems. No one can grow up acquiring every necessary psychological strength. A problem is merely a sign that you need to develop a new psychological strength.

Everybody has problems; don't bother about them. This misconception is the opposite of the previous one, but is equally paralyzing because it allows you to go along with your weaknesses without wanting to change them. Although it is true that everybody has problems, it is certainly not true that we should ignore them and their hidden strengths. Developing new strengths and hidden strengths is not only important for solving problems but feels good in itself.

All psychological problems are caused by social and environmental conditions. Don't wait for things to get better before you do something about yourself. You can change your inner environment and your home and work environments in important ways, and you will enjoy making the changes.

SURVEY

For each major problem area we have surveyed two to three hundred people who are involved in our programs and are actively trying to improve their own psychological fitness. Their responses to our questions will show you how others feel about their problems. We suggest that as you read along, you also write in your fitness notebook whenever the advice has a particular, functional application for you. Use the ideas in this book to make your life better. Use them on your friends and at work. It's the way for you to begin to take action.

As you mind jog, you go beyond the limitations of the problem and into new areas of your personality. You begin to find that you have a new identity, an identity that grows out of the problem. The more that you allow yourself to explore your problems and find strengths and weaknesses, the sooner you can become psychologically fit. Fitness is an active process. And it comes from what you can know best—the strengths hidden in your problems.

THE KEY TO
SOLVING PERSONAL PROBLEMS

The key to successful problem-solving is a fit personality. Problems or troublesome situations are stimulating for the personality. Stop trying to figure out the solution to any of your particular problems and begin discovering what personality skills you have or don't have in any problem area. In the fitness philosophy you have to become a fitness expert. That means you can't wait for someone else to bring you the latest solution to your next problem. The best solution is living in a new way, using all of your personality dynamics.

Worrying: Worry Less and Concentrate More

One of the finest long-distance runners in the country is running in a prestigious race. His race strategy has worked out perfectly as he turns the final curve at the track. He glances over his shoulder. Another runner is there. Too close. Much closer than he had anticipated. His plan of coasting home to an easy victory is gone. He feels a rush of adrenalin, he hesitates for a split second, and then shifts into what he later tells reporters is "overdrive." He outdistances his opponent and breaks the current meet record for the mile.

The runner would have lost the race if he had delayed another half-second. Instead, the situation pushed him to his fullest potential. You can use your worries in the same way. When you begin to worry you have a surge of feeling. Shift that surge into psychological overdrive and you will feel like a winner. But if, instead, you downshift, you change a worry into a problem. An extended worry is an unfinished race. It doesn't give us the satisfaction of trying our best and finishing nor does it allow us to rest and do nothing.

Here is what Fred, an accomplished worrier, told us about his life.

LOSING WITH WORRIES

I liked to work. I would take on projects, begin them with excitement and conviction, but soon I'd lose my enthusiasm and drive. I would try to complete my work, but inevitably would begin to worry.

I would worry about whether it would be good enough. I often would be concerned that I didn't know how to do it "right." I'd sit and think about not getting it done. Of course this would lead to the worry of what I would do when my work wasn't finished. Over and over again my thoughts turned to some imagined evaluation of my work from outside of myself. This imagining what someone else might say or think kept me from making wholehearted efforts.

My worrying had a deeper aspect than just thoughts filled with hesitation. I would think I was different; that I could not do what others could do; that basically I was not capable.

Worries were thoughts that kept me from doing my best. They undermined my wanting to do things to the point where I would go through the motions but get nowhere. Worrying is very much like twiddling your thumbs—there is little movement and it accomplishes nothing.

Fred is always looking over his own shoulder, so he can't make use of the strengths that he has. Worrying is more than not taking action—it is taking action against yourself.

In the psychological fitness perspective we are teaching you to understand your worries from a new place and to use this vantage point to shift from running in circles to mind jogging. You can't stop worrying, but you can learn what to do to shift your worries from hesitations to actions.

THE HOW OF WORRYING

There is in reality no such thing as a worry. There is only the active psychological process of worrying. When a person is a constant worrier it means he is psychologically trying to exercise his personality—not realizing how ineffective the exercise really is. The more a person worries the more he gets accustomed to worrying. He tolerates not having a solution. A psychological exercise should lead to new and more strenuous exercises. A worrier is an expert at an exercise that has no outer goal—there is never real competition to test and see if the exercise is making him more fit. What worrying does is to take the place of getting the inner self and the outer self in better psychological shape.

HIDDEN STRENGTHS AND WEAKNESSES IN WORRYING

Worrying must be brought out into the open so that all the psychological energy that is being used in a negative pursuit (worrying) can be funneled into more positive directions.

The hidden strength in worrying is that it is a natural form of concentration. When someone learns to concentrate in a systematic way, he quickly begins surpassing the performance of someone who doesn't. One form of positive concentration is meditation. When you meditate you concentrate on something neutral or positive—a mantra or your love of the guru. But when you worry you concentrate only on negative things—a possible failure, illness, or accident. It is not surprising that meditation makes some people feel good, and worrying makes people feel bad. What is the same for both is the energy used in the form of concentration. If you can realize that you have an incredible ability to concentrate and you can use that for positive ends, you will have learned the hidden strength of worrying.

The weaknesses in worrying are treacherous. Basically, worrying is a holding in or a suppressing of a full response to any situation. It is like having a car engine racing while in neutral. Worrying gives you two messages at once—"be alert" and "stay put."

There are reasons worriers continue to worry. They have come to identify themselves with the worrying process. They have spent years developing the subtle nuances of worrying, the multiple reasons for worrying, the inflections of worrying —in short, they believe that they are what they worry. In the psychological fitness perspective we believe that no one need define himself so narrowly.

When people don't have the chance to use the psychological fitness perspective they often fail to recognize the consequences of their worrying. They don't look at the long-term results. Worrying over time leads to tension. In its earliest stages it is a form of natural and incomplete exercise; as it progresses it is no longer exercise but a habit that leads to personality deterioration. Worrying keeps you from feeling what it is like to use all your energy for positive and effective ends. Worrying keeps you thinking about the outside while never taking the time to assess the toll of inner deprivation. Mind jogging helps you make the switch from negative to positive, from weaknesses to strengths, from worrying to concentrating.

SURVEY RESULTS—WORRIERS
ON WORRYING ▼

We administered surveys to people in a current psychological fitness program and over 80 percent reported worrying several times every day. At least 90 percent also admitted being unable to stop their worries during some period in their lives. They reported bodily symptoms connected with worrying in the following order of intensity: tightness, fatigue, "the fidgets," diarrhea, aches and pains in body, and headaches.

What People Say

When asked about their own ways of worrying, some of the people in this program said the following things:

> I talk back and forth to myself and get tenser and tenser.   JANE

> I worried about everything including good things that would happen to me. I could never enjoy myself because I was either looking ahead and worrying, or looking back and worrying.   JANICE

> I worried about doing well on exams or speeches. I worried I would fail. I stopped taking care of myself; I didn't think of anything else.   LISI

> My worried thoughts go round and round in my head. One leads to another and I have no peace. I got into Zen because of its promise to give freedom from thoughts. When I worry a lot I get headaches. I often feel a slight, tense pain in my temples and eyes.
>   JUDY

> I used to worry about what people thought of me—if they saw me as lonesome—and I tried to cover it all the time and look like I had something to do.
>   MICHAEL

> I could not find a way out of worrying.   ALAN

> When I start to worry I can't seem to stop. My worries take on a life of their own. I can't stop from going over and over them time and again. All of my attention is focused on what I am worrying about.
>   BILL

> I would spend all my time worrying about what I was doing and what I should be doing. I always worried that I was going too slow, too fast, that I wasn't okay

—whenever I was with people I worried about what I'd say—that anything I said was stupid.

KAREN

I worried about my health, my emotional state, and that the government was out to get me. I thought there must be some answer to life and I was worried about whether I'd ever find it. I was very lonely—never really telling anyone exactly what I worried about.

BOB

Spend hours and days worrying about everything imaginable. I can explain it as a low-frequency hum always present in my head.   WENDY

CONCLUSION: FROM RUNNING IN PLACE TO MIND JOGGING

Worrying is running a race in place, one that never gets anywhere. When you begin mind jogging with your worries, they change into wants. Strange as that may seem—each worry is a disguised want, one that doesn't have enough psychological energy behind it to come completely to the surface. You only worry about something which has meaning for you.

Once your personality begins functioning up to its maximum, it becomes possible to experience the difference between what you want and how you are. If you want your children safe, that is a positive want. You can concentrate on it. You can express that want; you can take action; you can be clear about it; you can feel it; and you can make contact with your children. All of these actions feel good. When you stop using all your personality dynamics, a simple want becomes a worry. Mind jogging gives you the ability to turn each of your worries back into their natural state of wanting.

11

Shyness:
Riches in Reserve

The television studio is filled with people. The band is playing the theme song. The applause sign goes on. The host appears, smiling. He begins his monologue. He makes fifteen to twenty million people laugh each night. No one would ever suspect that he is shy.

Shyness, when viewed from the fitness perspective, can be a positive psychological characteristic. Athletes can give brilliant performances before 80,000 fans, but as soon as they step up to the interview microphone may not remember their own names. Are they stupid? Hardly. They are shy. Shyness is a psychological process—a very active process. It tells you just how comfortable you are at any moment with your inner and outer selves. When you are comfortable with yourself, when there is no conflict between your inner self and outer self, then you don't experience being shy. That is why so many can perform in athletics or on stage—it is their outer self performing a skill they have worked on for years.

Shyness is inner excitement. When your inner self and outer self are not in harmony and you get excited, you experience shyness. From the psychological fitness perspective we say that shyness is "frozen excitement."

Since most people don't know how to handle and express their excitement, when it happens they get shy. If they let this response become a habit, before long it takes less and less excitement to bring on shyness. Pretty soon almost any little thing will make them feel shy.

SHYNESS: A PERSONAL STORY
FROM SALLY

I always considered myself a shy person. I was afraid to be with a lot of people, and I did my best to stay away. I always believed people wanted something from me—whether it was a smile from my beautiful face, or a shoulder to lean on, or an ear to bend. I never felt totally safe with people—unless it was one of the few friends I was close to. I felt most at ease by myself. I loved to be alone—to listen to music, to read, to watch TV, to clean house. I never experienced loneliness or discomfort when I was just with myself. The only problem my shyness presented was this uncontrollable fear I experienced when I was around most people. I literally couldn't socialize. I felt clamped up and frozen. I felt extremely secure and self-confident when I was by myself. This security I kept hidden away when I was with people. All I became aware of was my insecurity.

The redeeming quality of shyness is that it keeps you in touch with your inner self. Shyness gives you the freedom of instant introspection. This look at your inner self tells you that you are more than a mirror reflection of the world outside. Shyness lets you know that you are alive inside even though you don't have the slightest idea how to begin getting all the inner life to the surface.

The worst thing you could do to yourself would be to try to stop being shy. If you are shy it doesn't mean there is anything wrong with you. You have spent years gaining an identity built around your shyness. It has served you well. We don't want you to give it up—we want you to begin mind jogging with your shyness. We want you to use your shyness as a way to psychological fitness.

THE HOW OF SHYNESS

Shyness is a very active process. Your personality responds to every event in your life. You learn that shying away from what was happening was a good behavior skill. Only later did you realize that being shy might not be what you wanted.

If you want to change your shyness, then you have available the potential for change. Your inner self actually knows how you can be. All that you are lacking are the personality skills to move toward rather than away from. When a situation occurs and you have a rush of feeling, you withdraw instead of moving forward. The how of shyness involves learning the skills you need to begin taking forward steps with each situation.

Keep in mind that your shyness is a *personality response* to any situation. The shy response is really an incomplete response. The first part is the taking in of what is happening, the paying attention to the inner self, but the connection between the inner self and the outer self is so weak that the response never gets completed. The more that you learn to complete your responses the more you will move from shyness to explicitness. Could it be that shy people know something they aren't saying?

MISCONCEPTIONS ABOUT SHYNESS

A shy person and other people often rationalize shyness by using misconceptions.

Still waters run deep. That is part of the image of shyness. We are almost led to believe that shyness is better than directness. But since shy people don't make very much contact in general, we end up inferring that they have feeling. And this rather common inference is actually not valid. Still waters can be as shallow as a puddle.

Shy people are extra sensitive. Remember that people put good and bad labels on other people when they are uncomfortable. One of the most common labels is that shy people are extra sensitive. Everyone is sensitive. We all have vulnerable parts. And everyone experiences moments of shyness. People who do not appear shy simply have other strengths that they use. They do not continually rely on shyness as a form of communication.

Silent people are strong. The strong, silent woman and the silent macho man are stereotypes from movies. Shy people don't feel strong, though they may have a "better than other people" self-image. Strength is when you use what you have. A shy person can begin to really feel strong when he starts using what he has.

Women are more shy than men. That is not the case at all. Men and women are almost equally shy. Our surveys actually show men reporting slightly more shyness than women.

The best thing to do with a shy person is to leave him alone. A shy person needs help from those around him. He can get help by talking about specifics and then about ideas and feelings.

HIDDEN STRENGTHS AND WEAKNESSES OF SHYNESS

The hidden strength in shyness is that the shy person has inner responses to every event that occurs in his life. The weakness is *that is all he has.* Since the shy person doesn't have the skills to give a complete personality response, he gives a withdrawing response. Shy people see and hear and experience what is going on. They just don't know how to say what they already are thinking and feeling in private.

Since the shy person has not developed enough strengths to help him give the responses he does have, he begins to attack the main strength he has—his shyness. He begins to try to get rid of his excitement so that he won't be shy.

THE HIDDEN STRENGTH

Alan was a teacher in a junior college. When he was teaching in front of large classes he was cool and in control. He would tell jokes and interweave his lectures with personal anecdotes. He was as successful as he wanted to be in his career. But in his personal life he felt possessed by a demon. The minute he stopped lecturing he would feel so shy that he could hardly keep from running out of class. His forehead would break into tiny beads of sweat, his heart would start on a pounding rampage, his vision would narrow down. If a student would come up to visit with him he could hardly speak. He was always able to prepare himself for his performance, but afterwards it was disaster.

Alan tried everything to cure his shyness. He tried self-hypnosis. He tried tranquilizers but he got too sleepy during the lectures. Nothing worked, because it was one of his greatest strengths. It kept him in touch with his inner self.

Alan never overcame his shyness. Instead, he began mind jogging. We taught him to begin expressing more and holding in less. One day during a big lecture when he was masterfully illustrating a point—he stopped and looked out at the class. "I want you all to know that I love doing what I am doing. I get excited when I lecture. I want you to understand what I am teaching you. I love it."

He kept breaking down the rules of what a teacher could or couldn't say. He was learning how to stop running in place with his excitement and begin mind jogging.

Shy people think and talk to themselves, but they cheat themselves when they don't share their insights and excitement. A shy person is a person with hundreds of things to say. They are gabbers at heart. Every time they hold in what they think, they are keeping a weak muscle underdeveloped. Mind jogging is the psychological exercise for developing that muscle.

RESULTS OF TWO SHYNESS SURVEYS ▼

Professor Zimbardo and his colleagues at Stanford University administered a shyness survey to almost 5,000 people. They found that 80 percent of the people reported they were "very shy" at some time in their lives. They estimate from their survey results that four out of every ten Americans are shy—that is eighty-four million people!

One of the most interesting discoveries we made in our own shyness survey was that many people, both men and women, experience some form of shyness daily. Fifty-three percent of those polled reported feeling some sense of shyness more than once per day. And 79 percent said that at one time in their lives they were very shy—a shyness lasting for years!

We also asked people if they had the potential to change their own shyness and 92.3 percent said yes, they did. And 88.5 percent answered yes, that they had the potential to help someone else change his shyness. That statistic helps us understand that beneath the exterior of shyness is the power of insight and change. This is not surprising since the participants overwhelmingly agreed that family upbringing was the primary cause of their shyness.

The person with whom they were the most shy was with a friend of the opposite sex. And *second most* was with a friend of the same sex. The situation in which they felt the most shy was in a large group.

The top three physical symptoms associated with shyness were: first, tightness in the body (71 percent); second, fidgeting (58 percent); and third, poor coordination (38 percent).

What People Say

Here are some things shy people told us about shyness:

Whenever I am in a position to get attention from a few people, I get scared and sometimes forget what I want to say, or feel I can't go through with it—I feel like hiding.   ELIZABETH

I got extremely uncomfortable around people. I got embarrassed quite easily and tongue tied and flushed. I wanted to get away and disappear.   KEN

Felt scared to talk to acquaintances at work. Hid in my office. Avoided human contact. Got still.
                                        DAVID

I could hardly look anyone in the eye. I thought that I wasn't worth knowing, I put everyone above me.
                                        PATTY

I never looked at or had contact with anybody for fear of being hurt or seen.   DEBORAH

I was afraid to talk to people and have people talk to me. I was afraid I'd make an ass of myself and be laughed at. I would often just go completely blank when people talked to me and not know what to say. I also thought people wouldn't listen to me.
                                        DIANE

Up until my early twenties, I was very shy. I couldn't even talk on the phone. If I had to tell someone something personal, I'd write a letter.   MARTY

I would be too shy to say anything or even ask directions.   PAUL

I was the type that was so terrified I'd smile and talk right through but not feel a thing.   BARBARA

CONCLUSION: A NEW SOLUTION

The shy person withdraws feelings before he has said what he thinks. That flushing and burning sensation people often get when they experience being shy is the feeling of the with-drawal. The feeling is your body expressing inwardly what you don't allow yourself to say. If you can identify that experience for yourself you have begun to know the power that lies beneath.

In the psychological fitness approach you first identify that you are withdrawing *something*. You have ideas, responses, and feelings that you are withdrawing. You have something of value; you have to admit that. You can admit it just to yourself at first. But you must admit it.

The question you need to ask yourself is, "Do I want to keep holding back all my valuables?" A shy person is then being less than he really is. Admit to others, "I have something of value."

In order to develop the potential strength of feeling and awareness behind your shyness you have to pay attention to your outer self. That means paying attention to the little things that *you* have to say, paying attention to the things *you* feel. Start talking about yourself to someone else. Soon you will develop more trust and more independence. You will then feel all right getting attention in public and in front of people. You will allow yourself to be singled out for special attention because you feel special to yourself.

Most people mistakenly think the opposite of shyness is extroversion. It is not. The opposite is friendliness. You do not need to talk loud and be gregarious to overcome your shyness. The basic change is that you become friends with yourself. Then you feel friendly toward other people.

As you become friends with yourself, you will find a new identity. When you are your own friend your inner self emerges and blends with your outer self. You don't give up your excitement, you learn to enjoy and use it. Mind jogging allows you the freedom to exercise and attain your psychological fitness. You are no longer controlled by your limitations.

Shyness is something to be proud of—you have more riches than you knew about. In some ways you have been a miser with yourself. Your inner wealth is infinite—so you can start spending your ideas, and feelings, and excitement every day.

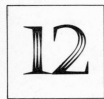

Loneliness:
From Private to Personal

Since the age of six she has been swimming. She swims because she wants to compete. She wants to go to the national
and international meets. She wants to win. More than anything she wants to go to the Olympics. Her swimming doesn't
leave much time for friends and lovers. In many ways she is
a lonely person. She knows that the loneliness comes from
swimming.

The loneliness of dedication is different from the loneliness
felt by people who just remain alone. When loneliness is not
used as a starting place or as a training ground for contact,
the person is not a psychological athlete.

JUDITH

She was going to be a great actress. There were thoughts
of riding around in a new Rolls Royce driven by a
chauffeur. But that was when she was twenty-five. At

thirty she was into dance, poetry, and writing music. Her apartment was bare except for a piano. She had three cats and worked herself hard. She had no friends. She feared rapists and birth control pills. Everywhere she looked there was danger. She had gone through seven abortions and still had no steady man in her life. But if you suggested that everything might not be fine, she would fight you tooth and nail, insisting that she was doing what she wanted. She was suffering from loneliness but she couldn't admit it. Psychologically she was desperate. Once every six or seven months she called an old girlfriend from high school. In a brittle, joking voice she would kid, "You know I only call you when I'm desperate."

The swimmer tests her training to see if it is getting her what she wants. At the same time she knows that her victories and records will pass. She can be number one for only a short while. The athlete knows that victories become memories. Lonely people don't have victories.

Loneliness can be dangerous. It increases your chances of dying early. Research has shown that premature death is far higher among the widowed, divorced, separated, and single. Dr. James Lynch shows in his book *The Broken Heart* that people who live alone are more likely to have heart attacks, cancer of the lungs, strokes, cirrhosis of the liver, and tuberculosis; there is also a higher incidence of suicide among them. The number of people practicing loneliness, the number and percentage of people living alone, is increasing.

Dr. Bruce Welch, a psychiatrist at Johns Hopkins University, found chemical changes and hormone changes in both isolated animals and men. He said, "They are prone to inability to act socially, to make bonds socially, and sustain them. This sets up a vicious cycle in which they are alone, become hyporeactive, become more rejected and become more alone. It has a feedback effect—loneliness making more loneliness."

No athlete in the world uses training methods that make him less able to compete. But that is just what loneliness does. There is nothing romantic about it. We are going to teach you how to find that hidden power in loneliness and use it to make yourself a psychological athlete.

LONELINESS IS A SKILL

Loneliness doesn't just happen. It is a psychological skill that people develop to survive, one of the few that we can develop entirely on our own. Many people have mastered it to near perfection. But like any single personality skill it is not enough in itself for fitness.

Eventually everyone *needs* other people. Judith, the woman whose life we described at the beginning of the chapter, mastered her skill of loneliness at an early age. By the time she was eight her mother had been in and out of numerous institutions because of chronic alcoholism and attempted suicide. Twice, before Judith was eighteen, her mother had tried to kill her. Judith's loneliness skill was a great psychological strength—she needed it to survive. It became a weakness only because she didn't have other skills to go with it.

The loneliness perspective can give you a sense of who you are. It gives you some control over yourself and the events in your life. And finally, it gives you an awareness of your identity. You can value yourself even when no one around you cares.

This strength loses its constructive side when it becomes a passive waiting, the dark side of wanting. You begin to lose the wanting, the connection to the real world. Although loneliness can give you a view of your interior world and tell you that you exist, wanting is what gives you contact with the real world.

How Loneliness Came to Be

Loneliness is a way of being which some children learn to use to keep their own inner sense of themselves. Loneliness develops when the child's inner sense of self is much stronger and more positive than his outer self. Lonely people have little sense of their outer identity, of how they seem to others.

A sense of identity develops when people respond to your outer self in a way that matches the way you feel on the inside. You can say to yourself,

> "I'm this kind of person."
> "People like this about me."
> "People don't like this about me."

When you have a definite feeling about yourself you feel good about meeting people.

The roles that we develop as children give us what we need, but at the same time they may force us into identities we do not necessarily want. If Judith, in our example, could come to understand *how* she creates the loneliness, then she could use her understanding to help change her life. That is the key to psychological fitness. The processes that we used as children to make our world make sense must now be used to make our world more fit. Judith needs to develop the weak areas of her personality and life.

Lonely people like Judith are not shy. They just can't find outside relationships which match their relationships with their inner selves. Loneliness can help you center yourself. But if you aren't careful it may keep you on dead center, unable to move.

THE HOW OF LONELINESS

We said earlier that staying alone gives a person a sense of intimacy with his inner self. That sense is a skill and a strength. We think it is a vital skill. But it is a skill that needs to be put into competition. An athlete only sits and prepares mentally after he has trained physically for his particular event and just before he begins competition. A lonely person has taken himself out of the running. When a lonely person begins mind jogging, he develops completely the skill of intimacy.

When you are lonely, you are stuck in an intimate relationship with yourself. But when you are "lonely with someone else" you are able to share intimacy in a very active way.

The more that you share your loneliness the more your entire personality benefits. Intimacy between you and yourself can become narcissism, but intimacy between you and another person is love. Love stretches and expands your personality.

LONELINESS IS A SIGNAL

Loneliness becomes a strength when you can use the level of intimacy, and honesty, and truthfulness with yourself as a barometer for outside relationships. You begin to know what you want with the people around you. You don't have to settle for a relationship that is superficial. You have an awareness from your loneliness that you want to relate at a certain level. When you make contact at that level you understand the power and the beauty of your loneliness.

If Judith could use her loneliness skills to move out into the world and make contact, she would find that she could have relationships that matched that sense of trust, autonomy, and intimacy that she experiences when she is alone.

In the psychological fitness approach, loneliness is used as a signal that you are drifting apart from people in your life. If you get that sense of separation, you are lonely.

Loneliness is a social disease for which there is a definite cure: friendship. When you are lonely it means you want and yearn for something more. It means you are alive.

MISCONCEPTIONS ABOUT LONELINESS

There are some common misconceptions about loneliness that need to be corrected.

Loneliness is a bad thing, a sign of psychological feebleness. As we have tried to show, loneliness can be a very powerful and good thing. It is a form of auto-therapy. A time when people work out thoughts about themselves and the world. Loneliness can be a centering, a time of finding yourself when the world around you is going too fast, an emotional time out.

Loneliness is necessary for creativity. This is one of the biggest myths about creativity—the suffering artist who needs loneliness in order to create. If an artist has the skill of making friends he can have his art and his life too.

Loneliness makes you deep and strong. Loneliness is a powerful psychological tool. For those who know how to use it, it is constructive; for those who are its victims, it is destructive.

If you can't be alone, you don't like yourself. This is a fine myth. It is a fine rationalization for people who can't make and keep close friends. But being alone doesn't mean you like yourself. A person demonstrates that he really likes himself when he is willing to show who he really is. There is only a certain amount of strength to solitude. When you can be with others and reveal yourself, new strengths are added to you.

One thing that lonely people seldom do is admit that they are lonely. Instead they say, "I'm not lonely, I'm just a private person." "I'm a loner." "I'm a lone wolf."

Ask yourself these five questions to find out if your loneliness is a personality weakness:

		YES	NO
1.	Do you spend time alone when you really want company?	——	——
2.	Do you give up wanting people to be with because you believe you can never have them?	——	——
3.	Do you turn down invitations because you are afraid?	——	——
4.	Have you resigned yourself to life alone?	——	——
5.	Do you fantasize being with people more than you are actually with them?	——	——

If you answered yes to two or more of these questions you are *very* lonely. The first step you can take toward fitness is to admit the truth to yourself.

THE HIDDEN STRENGTHS
AND WEAKNESSES OF LONELINESS

We have already told you the hidden strength of loneliness. It is the intimacy with your inner self. Loneliness is a natural form of mind jogging; it makes your inner self get in shape and come alive. The weakness of loneliness is that your privacy becomes more important to you than it should. You forget that it is possible to be intimate and personal with people rather than alone.

Your inner self needs to be tested and brought out into the light, or it becomes rigid. Loneliness is a skill of inner activity that is missing its counterpart: the skill of outer activity.

Your personality has such a strong drive for balance between your inner and outer selves that it turns on the lonely inner self. You begin attacking yourself to make your inner self less, to bring it back into balance. The attack also is the personality's way of trying to get you to take outside action. It is literally driving you out of yourself.

When you are lonely, energy builds up in your psychological system, and then must be used. If you don't have the necessary skills to use that energy for activity outside, you turn it inside, and the inner conflict begins. But turn it outside, and you become more personal and intimate with people and thus strengthen your overall personality. You use your ability to be personal to create an inner-outer mind jogging.

SURVEY RESULTS ON LONELINESS ▼

Over 75 percent reported that they felt lonely daily. A little more than 73 percent reported that their loneliness had lasted for years. But 99 percent said they felt they had the potential to become less lonely and 97 percent agreed they also had the potential to change someone else's loneliness. When asked what they thought was the cause of their loneliness over 70 percent related it to family upbringing. The four most reported physical symptoms were fatigue (72 percent), physical immobility (69 percent), numbness (45 percent), and aches and pains (40 percent).

Lonely People Talk about Loneliness

Here are some comments people gave us about loneliness:

> I would sit in my bedroom late at night after everyone was asleep and look out my window and cry. I would imagine getting a boyfriend and getting married and then I thought I'd be happy.
>
> DANA

> I was always lonely and away from people. Sometimes when I had too much to drink I would open up and talk a lot and not feel lonely.   NANNELL

> Did not talk to people. Stayed in my room reading books on how to live better.   ELKE

> I have always felt very much alone. Like I was very private way down inside myself and no one could see me. I have felt this way ever since I can remember. Like I don't really show who I am.   CATHY

> I was angry and bitchy. I didn't like or deeply care about anyone. I thought everyone was stupid and insensitive. I felt very tense most of the time.
>
> CAROLE

> I felt sad a lot. I sang songs in the dark. I felt like crying. I played the piano late at night. I climbed trees.
>
> SHERRY

> No matter what I would do to try not to be lonely it would not work. I would be happy for a very short time and then be lonely again.   GEORGE

> I grew up in a tough neighborhood and had to fight a lot. I felt very lonely and alone. It seems like I always felt that way.   BOB

> I was living alone and isolated myself from people and was very protective of my privacy. I tried to ignore that I was alone and very lonely and tried to believe

that I really didn't need people in my life and that I was okay being alone. I would daydream a lot about being around people and having friends. I would read or watch TV a lot. I usually waited for people to come to me and often pushed them away when they would attempt to get close.   DIANE

I didn't know then that I was lonely. I just felt like something was wrong.   ELLEN

DEBORAH'S STORY

For years, Deborah thought there was something "wrong" with her—she thought she was different. She would sometimes feel lonely while with her friends. She never talked to anyone about this. She was convinced that it simply proved that she didn't have any close friends, so she'd move on to new people and new situations.

For a while she'd be excited, but soon that familiar feeling of loneliness would be back and the cycle would start again. She finally stopped moving on. She started telling her friends whenever she felt lonely. And her friends took the time to listen and talk to her. She stayed. She found out there was nothing "wrong" with her, that she wasn't different.

Deborah has stopped living the life of a loner. She's started sharing her life with her friends. She knows that when she *thinks* there's something wrong with her it's because she isn't telling anyone how she feels. And when she does *share* her feelings, especially her loneliness, she finds her life is filled with friends.

CONCLUSIONS

A psychologically fit person uses his loneliness as a skill to help himself keep perspective. But he doesn't allow the loneliness to be a distorted view of the world. We are animals of contact. Through contact we make sense out of the depth we experience in our loneliness.

When loneliness becomes as active as it is deep, it stirs your psychological waters. You are no longer placid and deep. You are deep like the ocean, moving and alive. That is what mind jogging your loneliness can do for you. It can give you a new sense of identity, an inner depth which you can share with those in your world.

When your identity is controlled by your loneliness you are half an identity. But you can use that half as your first half step to mind jogging. By mind jogging you will move from a private sense of identity to a public sense of identity, and both will be personal and intimate.

From Guilt to Innocence

Everyone experiences guilt. But very few people experience "positive guilt," which is an invigorating and self-stimulating psychological exercise, as opposed to negative guilt, which is debilitating and depressing.

Negative guilt occurs when you lose contact with your inner self. Your outer self is then forced to rise all alone to meet the requirements that you have set for it. The logic of negative guilt is that whatever you do is wrong.

Positive guilt is a self-awareness. It means that you accept what you are doing. You remember that you have chosen it, and you want to do it as well as you can. Your guilt feelings can then teach you—their logic is that what you are doing is right even though it isn't perfect. When you are able to re-establish contact between your inner self and outer self, then you can begin using positive guilt.

With negative guilt you keep berating yourself for what you have done wrong. With positive guilt you check on yourself to see if you are using your potential. If you are not, your positive guilt shows that you have more energy than you are using and signals what more you can do.

Positive guilt is what you use for your psychological peak performances, a way of asking yourself what you want to do.

Negative guilt stops you. It moves you away from the zone of peak performances—to hesitation, self-doubt, and disharmony. When you begin mind jogging you will find that guilt naturally and easily becomes positive. You will learn how to reassure yourself and at the same time maximize your potential. Your inner self and outer self won't be at war.

Some people think they could never live without guilt. We are not asking you to give up guilt but merely to change it from negative to positive guilt.

The How of Guilt

We have emphasized positive guilt as negative guilt turned inside out. There is another aspect to think about. Guilt only occurs after something has happened. You can experience guilt with almost any feeling. You can be having a wonderful time, and if you don't know how to express it, you can wind up feeling guilty because guilt is the residue of feeling. That is why the how of guilt is actually the way that we express ourselves. Athletes feel guilty about their performance when they don't perform up to their potential. We experience the same feeling in any situation in which we don't perform up to our maximum. Guilt is what is left over.

When we do something less than we are able to do we feel guilt. This is what makes positive guilt so important. It gives us immediate feedback. Are we using as much energy as we want to be using? When we are not, it means we are not experiencing all that we could. Expression is a key to releasing ourselves from guilt; guilt means we are not expressing what we are experiencing.

You can test yourself to see if you usually use positive or negative guilt. Answer these five questions with a yes or a no:

		YES	NO
1.	Do you usually apologize even if you may not be in the wrong?	___	___
2.	Do you brood about what went wrong for days on end?	___	___
3.	Do you always try to change when people don't like the way you do things?	___	___
4.	Do you usually try to anticipate what others will like or dislike?	___	___
5.	Do you try to replay things that can't be changed over and over in your head?	___	___

If you answered yes to two or more of the questions, you definitely need to learn to use your guilt feelings in a positive way.

Marilyn's score on the little test showed she was an expert in negative guilt.

MARILYN'S STORY

How I Learned to Feel Guilty in Many Hard Lessons

All the time I was growing up—except for some clear instances that stand out—I just didn't like being with my mother. I didn't like for her to touch or kiss me. I would tense up. When I came home from school, I'd try to sneak past her and get to my room, or I'd be glad she was asleep so I wouldn't have to talk to her.

When I was young—and even into my teens—there were always horrible fights in my house, mainly between my mother and brother. Even though I was the youngest, I tried to arbitrate in those fights. I tried to fix things up in my family so everyone would feel good. I didn't feel good.

I always wished I had a different mother. I'd compare mine to other mothers. I liked my best friend's mom a lot and would spend a great deal of time at her house because I felt good there. They didn't fight.

When I was twelve, my mother came to visit me at

camp. After she left, my girlfriend said to me, "Boy, you sure don't treat your mother very nice." I felt bad and embarrassed. I decided to treat my mother better. I felt very guilty about my feelings toward my mom and how I treated her. I didn't know what she had done to me to deserve such hatred in return.

I would really try to be nice. But there would be times that I would sit across from her and fantasize hurting her. When we'd argue, I'd always end up going in her room and apologizing. I'd feel a little better after doing that, but then I'd start hating her again, my fantasies would begin, and I'd feel guilty again. I would torture myself with thoughts that I was evil—a bad, unloving daughter. I thought I was not capable of loving anyone, and that I would actually contaminate people who got close to me.

My mother criticized me and my brother all the time. My hair was too long, my skirts were too short, I didn't see enough of some people and I saw too much of others, why couldn't I be like so-and-so? She especially compared me to girls who "did things for their mothers." This added to my guilt.

Marilyn never realized that she was doing what she had trained for years to do. Unfortunately, negative guilt wasn't working for her. Even though she wanted to change she didn't have the skills she needed to begin mind jogging with positive guilt.

Guilt is an incomplete way of interacting with yourself and with someone else. When someone tries to make you feel guilty it means they want something more from you. And when you make yourself feel guilty it means you want something more. When you haven't expressed what you want or done what you want, then you feel negative guilt. It is always concerned with what has passed.

Positive guilt concerns what is happening in the present. When someone expresses positive guilt he tells you what he wants in time for you to respond to him. When you allow yourself to feel positive guilt, you are immediately aware of wanting more and are ready to take action. The event is still occurring. Positive guilt is about what is happening.

SOME MISCONCEPTIONS ABOUT GUILT

Guilt is good for people. It helps to control them. Guilt usually doesn't control what people do, it only makes them feel bad while they do what they want to anyway.

Guilt is good for you. Guilt does not make you stronger, smarter, wiser. All that guilt does for you is to make you unhappy in what you are doing.

If you feel guilty you have done something wrong. The guilt you feel only means you haven't understood what your potentials are.

Guilt is what most people suffer from. People don't suffer from guilt. They suffer from not saying yes and no. Guilt is the middle ground—the place to be neither happy nor unhappy.

Other people make me feel guilty. It is true that you were taught how to be guilty when you were young. But now you are doing it yourself. No one can lay it on you anymore.

A HIDDEN STRENGTH

In the previous chapter we talked about loneliness as a signal that a person needs and wants more intimacy. The hidden strength in guilt is that it is a barometer of what you can *do*. When you have a feeling or sense of guilt you have become aware of your unanswered and unused potentials.

It is impossible to feel guilty if you are doing everything that you can. If you know that you have done your utmost, then you cannot be shaken. But if you haven't maximized your potential, then you are susceptible to guilt.

Here is how the weak aspects and the strong aspects of guilt might appear.

Weak Aspects	Strong Aspects
I'm not doing what you want	I might
I shouldn't	I want something more
It was all my fault	I want something different
I should be a better person	I understand it differently now

Why didn't I think of that? I want to do better
I should have known better I want to change
I keep thinking about it I want more responsibility
Everyone will dislike me I want people to like me
This is wrong I want to feel good
This is bad I want to change it

TWO SURVEYS OF GUILT ▼

In a recent survey taken in *Psychology Today* 32 percent of the men and 36 percent of the women who were sampled said they had "frequent guilt feelings as children."

When we asked the participants in our fitness programs about guilt, 33 percent of the men and 26 percent of the women reported feeling guilty several times a day as adults. A total of 79 percent of these same people said they experienced periods of guilt in their past that lasted for days, weeks, months, and even years. The top three bodily symptoms they experienced during periods of guilt were: body tightness (85 percent), fatigue (47 percent), and fidgeting (49 percent). These symptoms and others that were reported all reflect a held-in body.

What People Say about Guilt

I would want to punish myself for bad things and would punish myself physically.   JOHN

I felt awful if I didn't follow rules like "Be Nice." I experienced guilt for years after leaving home and not going to college.   GARY

When I lost my baby I thought I was not living my life the "best" way or I had done something wrong somewhere along the way that God could punish me for.
ELIZABETH

I felt guilty about wanting to go away to school because my father had no money to send me.

LYNN

I felt very guilty about my mother's death and thought
I could have changed what happened.   MARK

My mother would act hurt constantly and act as if I
had brutalized her. I always felt as if I were cruel and
everything I did was hurtful to others.

RICHIE

I would just feel awful and think I was the worst person in the world. I couldn't look anyone in the face.

DANA

I used to think that everything was my fault. I was
told that as a kid. When anything would go wrong at
work or even to the extent of traffic jams, I would
think I caused the trouble.   ALAN

CONCLUSION

When guilt is the medal you keep pinning on yourself for
your actions, you begin to stop wanting to compete at all. You
begin to see everything from the viewpoint of a psychological
loser. Everything is always seen as what is wrong. Negative
guilt controls you and limits how you can be and what you
can do. Positive guilt increases the pace of your mind jogging.
It gets you going and keeps you moving toward your potential. It is you letting yourself and the people around you
know what you want and how you think things can be.

Two Special Mind Jogs for Guilt

Mind Jog One. Guilt is not much fun. In this mind jog you
have to exaggerate your guilt to the point where it becomes
ridiculous. Start by saying, "I feel guilty about ———— "
and fill in the content. Then shift to a confession.

"I confess I haven't —————————
    I shouldn't —————————
    I didn't —————————," etc.

Then go one step further. "I confess I am the worst" (son, mother, worker, and so on). By the time you extend your guilty statements to this point they should feel a bit ludicrous. You will have changed a melodrama into a bad-guy comedy.

Mind Jog Two. Make up a guilty or innocent chart. Do you usually consider yourself guilty until proven innocent or innocent until proven guilty? Most people who suffer from strong guilt feelings act as though they are guilty until proven innocent. Start acting as your own lawyer. Insist on your innocence. Every time you find yourself pleading guilty, change your plea to innocent.

Blame:
It's Only Half the Story

The national collegiate basketball championship game is tied. The two best teams in the country are matched man for man. The coach calls for a certain play. He tells each of his players exactly what he wants him to do. He emphasizes, "Avoid fouling any of the other players." There are only fifty-eight second left. The star guard tries a spectacular steal and fouls the man he is defending. The opposing player goes ahead and scores. The coach calls time out. He looks at his guard. "I didn't want you to do that, but it happens to the best of us. We've got plenty of time." The next play the guard shoots a basket and is fouled. A three-point play. Time has run out. The player who just fifty-eight seconds ago was the goat is now a champion. He is the game hero.

The real hero of the game was the coach. He could have berated his player for making a dumb mistake. The player was obviously doing that to himself already. Instead, he clearly said the obvious: "I didn't want you to do that," and then he went on to help his player give his best.

Blaming is really the first half of teaching. When you blame someone you often forget that you want something from them. It is a good thing to want from other people. But when you don't get it and you blame them, you are actually moving farther away from getting what you really want.

When you righteously blame someone, even yourself, you separate your inner self, which is hurt and disappointed and wanting more, from your outer self, which sounds sure about what is right and what is wrong. If you give half an answer you are never going to get what you want. The inner self's answer—"I am hurt" or "I am disappointed" or "I want so much more"—is not a fit answer because it is not complete, any more than is the outer answer—"you are late," "you are wrong," "you shouldn't have." When your answer reflects both selves, you have become a teacher.

When you combine the inner response with the outer response you have a powerful tool for teaching. If you take the time really to tell someone else what you want and how you feel, he or she will often do the same with you.

Many people hate themselves for blaming because it is such a negative behavior. But they can't stop. We have had mothers in our programs who totally break down, crying and sobbing, when they talk about blaming their children, husbands, and themselves. They can't stop blaming because they want to make the world around them a better and more pleasant place to be and to express what happens to their inner selves.

Every time you lay blame, the inner self is using the outer self, but in a disguised way, so it isn't effective. Then you begin to believe blaming is the only way you can be close to your inner self, without realizing that all the time you are trying to exercise your inner self. That is why your attempts to control yourself are often fruitless. You want your inner self to emerge and harmonize with your outer self, and think blaming helps you achieve this.

THE HOW OF BLAMES

Blaming is an interesting psychological phenomenon because you are giving only half a response to a situation, and it makes you feel bad because you are not using all of your potential.

Looking at your behavior from the fitness perspective helps you move toward more growth. But blaming stops you and moves you toward less. Blaming stops the interaction between two people. "You are wrong and I am right." Yet what every blamer really wants is to move beyond blaming. The coach in the example knew how to do this. He knew the mind jogging for blaming because he gave his player a way out.

It is our belief that everyone wants to do his best. When he does something wrong he shows that he needs to learn more skills in how to do something right.

If someone blames you, you react. But if you have done something wrong, which everyone does at different times, you are more than willing to hear what you can do differently and how what you did affected someone else.

Any learning you do to express both your inner self and outer self is a good exercise for your personality. It always makes you a stronger and more psychologically fit person.

MISCONCEPTIONS ABOUT BLAMING

People get what they deserve. This is the major justification for blaming. Blamers tend to believe they are just telling the truth. It isn't enough just to state facts. You must recognize and respond with feelings.

When something goes wrong it's got to be somebody's fault. Blamers tend to live in a psychological world that is as fixed and definite as Newtonian physics: For every action there must be someone to blame. Something can go wrong and be no one's fault—it can just go wrong. And something can look wrong to one person and right to another.

There is always a right and a wrong way to do something. This misconception certainly simplifies life and causes arguments. People who believe this will often accompany their blaming with statements like "It's for your own good" and "Everybody knows" and "I just want you to know what is right."

If you don't blame someone else you will have to blame yourself. It is true that when blamers don't have anyone to blame they will often blame themselves. It is false that they have to blame.

THE HIDDEN STRENGTHS AND WEAKNESSES OF BLAMING

The hidden strength of blaming is the intense feeling. The blamer strongly wants something and strongly cares about what happens. But frequently blamers don't talk about what they really want or what they care about most. Instead they approach things indirectly.

Every blamer wants very strongly to feel good. But he will often settle for feeling anything, as long as it is strong. Every blamer usually finds a blamee. The blamer needs and wants the blamee, and the blamee needs and wants the blamer.

JANE'S STORY

One woman in her early twenties complained that she was unable to maintain a relationship with a man: "I was constantly blaming anyone I was involved with or wanting to be involved with for not returning my love. I was desperate to try to hold on to someone and at the same time the only reason I could think of for why I didn't have what I wanted was that one guy after another was 'afraid to be loved, afraid to be close, unable to love,' etc., etc. If only HE would come through, then I would be happy and have just what I wanted. I tried desperately to prove my point to one him after another, to show him the error of his ways. I couldn't understand why my relationships were just one fight after another, or why guys always wanted to get away when all I wanted was

to love them and be loved. But I knew it wasn't my
fault. Even in high school, when my boyfriend would do
anything that was different from what I wanted or expected, my attitude was that he was wronging me
terribly."

She was able to learn new ways to talk and make contact, to learn how to relate to people—not just boyfriends, but people in all types of relationships. She
learned how to stop blaming the other person for her
unhappiness and to have and share her own feelings—
of wanting, disappointment, hurt, excitement, etc. One
assignment she was given was to spend a half hour
a night telling her boyfriend how important he is to
her, what she likes about him, what happens to her when
she blames him and is not close to him, and what her
life would be like without him. She found out that what
she really wanted was to feel her own loving—that was
what was missing. She was blaming everyone else because she missed her own loving feeling.

Jane found that her hidden strength in her blaming was
her caring. She really cared about her boyfriend. But more importantly she cared about her own strong feeling. As she acquired the skill to fully express and live with that strong
feeling she became more psychologically fit.

Many mothers and fathers never recognize how their children resent the years and years of being blamed. If you blame
a child, he will either blame himself and buckle under, or he
will blame you and fight back. In either case neither parent nor
child is getting what he wants.

SURVEY RESULTS ON BLAMING ▼

We found a high percentage of reported blaming—78
percent reported blaming at least once a day, while 52
percent reported that they blame someone "several
times a day." This was true even though 61 percent
of the people reported that they were able to blame
less as a result of the program.

Another astonishing figure concerns how long blaming can go on. Of the 75 percent of the people who reported that they had "blamed excessively" during some period of their life, 52 percent said that their blaming had gone on for years.

The dominant physical symptom reported while blaming is tightness—89 percent of the people surveyed said they felt this. Three more notable symptoms were also reported: headaches (37 percent), fatigue (36 percent), and fidgeting (36 percent).

What People Say

Here are some things people told us about blaming:

I blamed my parents for my sexual problems. I blamed my sexual problems for my loneliness and depression. I liked having someone to blame; it seemed to ease my self-hate. STEVEN

I blamed my parents for what they had done to me. I blamed them silently like carrying a grudge. I didn't want to talk to them or give them any indication that I knew they existed. WENDY

I would feel that the way I felt was "their" fault and I wouldn't be satisfied till "they" felt as bad as I did, or I made them pay for what "they" did to me. BOB

I would never maintain friendships with people. I'd find something bad about them, or some way they'd turned on me and then stop being friends with them. I'd then try to talk other people into not liking them. BOB

I blamed the staff, my wife, the President, and anyone who wasn't in Vietnam for how bad I felt there, all my friends who died, and what I missed at home. JOHN

I would hold in and be angry, seething inside. I hated cops, teachers, parents, political leaders, wife.

JOEL

I was with a boyfriend who I was unhappy with. I became very critical of him, blamed his incompetence for my unhappiness. I would become very angry, throw tantrums (throw pillows and things), then feel guilty for not understanding my boyfriend and want to make up.   MARY

Being unhappy, I would blame my wife. I would remain passive and unhappy. I remember living in a complaining mood for months. The consequence was that nothing changed.   RON

CONCLUSION

Once blamers begin to move toward contact they start to experience something new—vulnerability. They find they want a lot in their relationships from the person they used to blame. They find they have many real things and complimentary things and vulnerable things to say. The bitterness of blaming is replaced by the sweetness of love and contact.

We want to introduce you to a new word—"bettering." The hidden characteristics we have described in blaming are intense caring, wanting, vulnerability. When you put all of these words into action you have bettering. A blamer is someone who has yet to learn the skill of bettering. We think that you have the right to make your own life better, you have the right to make your relationships better, you have a right to make the world better. Bettering is the active process of seeing something that you want to change and beginning to change it. When you are bettering, you are mind jogging.

When you are bettering you are blending your inner self and outer self for your own good. You are striving for your own potential. Blaming is an ineffective way of reaching for more in your life. Bettering means you are committed to your own and other people's well-being. When you are bettering you don't know the final destination. You take what you want to change, and admit it, and then you express how you feel about it. There is no game to win or lose. There is only the freedom of mind jogging. If you have more room than you need for a lifetime of mind jogging, you are bettering. But if you find your world getting narrower and more restricted, then you are blaming. Give your own desire for bettering a chance.

Frustration:
Starting Your Own Engine

"He's done it. He's broken the world record. Jenner is the new Olympic champion." Everyone has heard the stories about Bruce Jenner the winner. But no one seems to remember that for years he knew he had it in him to win, but didn't have the skills to do it. His frustration was no different from yours or anyone else's.

Frustration is defined in one psychology text as a "nearly inevitable result of conflict between the individual's wants and the restraints imposed by society." But what happens when frustration isn't due to society's restraints?

Let us stop calling frustration a problem. There is a positive strength hidden in frustration, which we will call striving. A frustrated person desires something more, a future and a direction in his life.

It is impossible to live without striving. Frustrating ourselves to create this striving is one of the most natural and intense forms of personality exercise that we can do. When we realize that it is the act of achieving we want, rather than the prize itself, then we understand frustration and how to use it.

When you choose to frustrate yourself, the process gives you energy to seek new solutions and to try out new personality strengths and explore new areas in your life. Frustration signals each person about his or her dissatisfactions.

The frustration genius. Some people who find themselves frustrated focus on what they are *not* getting, so they specialize in the act of never getting what they want. Their belief about themselves does not come from striving, but from stopping.

MICKEY'S PLAY

One of our patients had a play that he had been working on for twenty years. It was huge. He had built his entire life's frustrations around this play which he couldn't finish. He didn't pay attention to his weaknesses in sex, friends, play, work, and other areas. He thought that if he could get this play done he would be all right.

His entire progress was related to that play. We worked with him to produce it. He resisted with thousands of excuses, but finally he put on his play. It was a complete flop.

After the flop we told him to write little five-to-six-minute plays that involved both his feelings and his friends. He had to put on a play a week. Over the course of the year he had to change all his dynamics to get his plays produced. He was moving, talking, making contact, and sharing his feelings. By the end of the year he had freed up energy that was changing his relationships and the way he worked. He was striving in all areas of his life.

Mickey's story is much better than his play. Many people frustrate themselves with pictures of things they are going to be, but they don't test themselves. It was surprising to watch this man free up so much of his emotional energy that had been locked up in his picture of "the great play." Some of his short plays were terrible while others were smashing successes. He had audiences crying and laughing—often at the same time. No longer caught in frustration, he was using his striving. As he learned that he liked the feeling of *trying to write*, and the feeling of *trying to create*, he was able to find that feeling in many of the underdeveloped areas of his life. He began to love "trying to."

In the same way Bruce Jenner became the Olympic champion long before the final event of the decathlon. He became a champion when he used his frustration to strive for more. If Jenner has learned the real lessons from his frustration, he will continue to have that winning feeling which comes from striving for more. The same feeling that each frustration creates for you.

THE HOW OF FRUSTRATION

Frustra*ting* is good for us. But there is no such value to frustra*tion*.

Frustrating is an exciting process. Our inner self is constantly measuring our goals and potentials. But the inner self needs to exercise the outer self if the person is to become psychologically fit. In order to do this the inner self is constantly setting goals half an inch more than we can accomplish.

The key to mind jogging frustration is to accept the dynamic inner and outer process that occurs while we are frustrating. Frustrating is an intense and beneficial psychological exercise. It gives us hope that we can accomplish, and the knowledge that there is no accomplishment that will ever give us a greater fitness than the "accomplishing."

The process of frustrating is healthy for us. It gives us a dynamic sense of identity. We become someone who can reach and try. We don't have to win and succeed at everything because we are winning and succeeding in the trying. When your outer self accepts the inner need to exercise and strengthen your entire personality you gain a new awareness. You begin to enjoy and trust your frustrating. You use frustrating as a way to improve your mind jogging.

Mind jogging is a way of helping your inner self and outer self work together. You don't have to make yourself unhappy.

You can experience what it feels like to have an inner self that has a sense of where you want to go and an outer self that wants to go there. It is like finding you have your own army of friends.

MISCONCEPTONS ABOUT FRUSTRATION

People who are frustrated and stopped believe and practice some of the general misconceptions about frustration.

Frustration is when you don't get what you want. That is false. You might be disappointed and sad—but when you do everything that you can do to get something, then you are using your frustration. It is the wanting of something that feels good.

You can let your frustrations out physically. That is a big misconception. You can release tension and anxiety from frustrations, but they must be dealt with psychologically if they are to be resolved.

When you get what you want you will be completely satisfied. Every time you got what you wanted, after awhile, you shifted to something new. It is the process of trying to resolve your problems that satisfies, not the resolution.

It is somebody, or something, or some event that kept me from getting what I wanted. "If it wasn't for . . . I would have succeeded." If that sounds like you, you are missing out on a wonderful experience—the experience of knowing that you are the cause, the reason, and the benefactor of all that you do. It is impossible to fail. You only fail if you don't do anything. If you don't experience yourself frustrating yourself as a way of searching for new answers and new solutions and new feelings, then you will always be caught in frustration.

How Frustration Becomes a Strength

Frustration was never a total weakness. The hidden strength of frustration is that it signals the person about dissatisfactions.

Frustration is what we do to ourselves when we see the light at the end of the tunnel. You cannot frustrate yourself until you have a possible solution. You cannot frustrate yourself unless you know you can reach your goal. Does this mean that you are going to find or get exactly what you want? No. Psychological fitness is not simplistic. When you are frustrating yourself you are solving or working or desiring something more. You are giving yourself a future and a direction in your life.

It is possible to live without frustration, but it is impossible to live without frustrating ourselves. If there were no frustrating, then we would have no sense of our own time and future. It can make us more fit.

When you realize that you are choosing to frustrate yourself, and it is that process which gives you the energy to seek new solutions and to try out new personality strengths and explore new areas in your life, then you understand some of the most fundamental principles of psychological fitness.

The weaknesses of frustration occur when we don't get what we want. We begin to believe that what we wanted was too much, and that not getting it was the cause of our frustration. That is not true. You frustrate yourself because you need to. But if frustration is your only strength, then you begin to sabotage yourself by never allowing complete success. You create ways of stopping yourself from succeeding so that you can keep using your biggest strength—frustration.

Many people who want success and never get it often think that if they only had certain breaks, then they would make it. They are really kidding themselves. They are already successful at frustration. What they are afraid of is succeeding. Success would challenge their sense of identity—a sense they have been developing for years.

When a person learns to mind jog his frustration, then he knows how to change frustrating to creating and how to change waiting (for solutions) to solving. It is the difference between knowing how to use your psychological energy or leaving it up to chance. As you take responsibility for using your energy for your own good, you stop frustrating yourself with losses, and you begin winning in the world.

SURVEY RESULTS ▼

> When we asked 250 people how often they experienced being frustrated, 75 percent of them reported being frustrated daily, and 43 percent several times daily.
>
> Asked if at some time in their life they had been a very frustrated person, over 90 percent reported that they were. And when asked how long that frustration lasted, 52 percent of those who reported yes said it lasted for years.
>
> The main physical symptoms they reported were tightness in body (91 percent), fidgeting (71 percent), and fatigue (62 percent), with aches and pains and headaches both getting a 40 percent response.

What These People Say about Frustration

Here are the comments made by several of the people. Notice how the frustration hides the striving.

> I lay around dreaming pictures of what I wanted, and it seemed so far away. I didn't know how to get started.   BOB

> I believed that I could not effect any change on my environment. I felt helpless—unable to accomplish anything. I felt I couldn't change until things changed around me.   CAROLYN

> I felt dissatisfied. Nothing I did was satisfying—even things I did well. I didn't feel good inside.
>   MARY

> I was totally frustrated about a career. I was confused most of the time. I felt helpless and ineffective and fearful that I would end up in failure.
>   JERRY

I wanted to have friends but I focused on not having any, and I believed I couldn't have any.

NANCY

I was very unhappy and very negative. I wanted to change and tried things like yoga, chanting, dope, being intellectual, and dieting all the time.

JEANIE

I thought I would never make it as a mother and that my kids would never be happy and that they were suffering. I thought I'd never be able to be the right way with them.   ANN

I would be convinced that I could never have things the way I wanted—it was always out of my control and there was always something wrong.

LAURIE

Nothing was right—I kept trying—I felt angry—I focused on what was missing.   VINCENT

Three Special Mind Jogs for Frustration

Use one of these mind jogs the next time you feel especially frustrated.

Mind Jog One. Write your frustrations on several sheets of paper in big CAPITAL letters. Now rip the sheets into little pieces—make confetti. Toss the confetti up in the air and watch it float down. Everyone of those tiny pieces of paper represents a frustrating thought. Now start to pick each one up, but begin to change your thinking from "I can't" or "I haven't" to "I'm trying. . . ." Really tell yourself what you are trying to accomplish.

Mind Jog Two. Imagine that every one of your frustrations is a tiny pin prick that jabs at your desire. Very soon you will become deflated if you continue to jab at yourself. Now imagine that instead of jabbing and poking you begin to touch and pull yourself forward. Every time you think a frustrating thought, begin to massage your hands; do it gently so that you can start to feel the good wishes you have for yourself behind the frustration.

Mind Jog Three. Draw a line with an arrow at the end, like this ——————————➤. Now every time you feel frustrated, recognize that you are trying to point yourself and move yourself toward something. Keep a record of how many pointed lines you draw in a day. Begin to put some content in the lines by writing in an "I'm trying for. . . ."

————————————————————➤

CONCLUSION

These three special mind jogs are important pieces of advice. They tell you that you are trying to take care of yourself, and you are going somewhere. Mind jogging gives you the power to break down the psychological barriers against admitting you are trying to live your life as well as possible. You begin finding out just how exhilarating it is for your inner self and outer self to work together as you mind jog. The more you allow yourself the freedom of solving and creating and succeeding, the more you will find that solutions, and creations, and success are a natural part of your life.

16

The Blues:
From Depression to Expression

Dean Smith, basketball coach of North Carolina, worked on a tactical problem for years. His team is ahead by three points, but the opposing team has the momentum. How does he keep the lead and win the game?

Smith created the four-corner offense. Some coaches call it a slowdown. Smith made the clock work for his teams. He decided that he could win more games if he literally slowed down the tempo until his team had an easy basket. The widespread use of his methods tells you how successful the idea is.

Psychological depression is a way of slowing down. Many people think of depression as a solely defensive stance. That is not true. It is an offensive, or creative behavior.

When you are depressed it means you are responding to a situation in which your outer self has been unsuccessful. Your inner self then begins to depress the rules, regulations, and meanings that your outer self normally uses, making depression a form of mind jogging. When you are depressed, you are trying to bring your inner self and outer self closer together.

The National Institute of Mental Health reports that depression is replacing schizophrenia as the number one mental illness in the United States. It hospitalizes more than 125,000 people a year. Their report states that 15 percent of the population show signs of "serious mental depression."

At any given time from 25 to 40 percent of the population suffers from the milder forms of depression. We are not saying depression is an effective skill, but it is a skill that works to some degree or people would not use it. But because some skills are used and others remain undeveloped, it is not efficient.

THE HOW OF DEPRESSION

A relatively obscure French psychologist, Hubert Benoit, has developed a series of exercises that he uses to teach people how to depress positively. As the first part of his technique, he asks people to write meaningless but structured sentences. A typical sentence might be "I fly while walking in a chair to meet the door." If you write enough such sentences, you begin to realize that meaning in your life comes through social learning and not self-learning. His ideas provide an explanation of what depression does for us. We can see this more clearly if we break depression into three parts.

1) *First of all, we depress.* When you de-press, you no longer press. When you press you are moving and changing your life. When you are de-pressing you stop. You begin to withhold and withdraw. The question we ask in our fitness program is not "Why are you depressed?" or "What makes you depressed?" or "What is depressing?" but "How are you depressing?"

2) *We suspend meaning as we depress.* When we depress we refuse to believe that everything will turn out as we planned. We no longer pretend that the people around us are really talking to us. We stop expressing the conventional platitudes.

Depression is our test of the validity of our own experience and our own existence. We are left with no meaning, the conviction that "nothing means anything." When you have removed all your content, then you are left only with your inner self.

3) *We create new meanings when we depress.* Depression serves as a way for the personality to evaluate what means something to our inner self and what doesn't. If we were never depressed we would not know what feeling good meant. It allows us to reach the point of "I want to have as much positive meaning and pleasurable feeling as I have negative meaning and bad feeling when I feel depressed." We use depression to create new meaning.

Depression creates a crisis in which you test your personality strengths and weaknesses, and get to know how you are, rather than what you are supposed to be. When you decide to depress yourself, you are saying something very strong about yourself—"I am more important than all the social rules and regulations about keeping up a good front, talking a certain way, going along with what's expected, and all the old meanings."

MISCONCEPTIONS ABOUT DEPRESSION

Depression is part of a cycle that can't be avoided. Not true. Depression can be avoided. Once you learn how you *depress* you will have the tools necessary to keep renewing your life perspective.

Depression is a deep feeling. False. Depression is just that —a depressing of your feelings. It is only when you stop depressing yourself that you can begin to feel. Any feeling is better than depressing your feelings.

When depression hits, you have no choice—you are a victim. That is not true. We have found in our work that depression is a very active process.

When depressed, you have to wait until it passes. Tiredness, fatigue, helplessness are characteristic of depression. If you get depressed, one of the best things you can do is move.

Your body needs help to turn the depression into a creative experience.

You can cure depression with drugs. Being depressed is not cured by drugs. It can be *put off* by taking drugs, but it can end only when natural personality dynamics are used to reverse the process of depressing. Expression and activity need to take place if growth and expansion of the personality are going to occur.

THE HIDDEN STRENGTHS
AND WEAKNESSES OF DEPRESSION

Depression can work for you if you recognize that there is some strength in what you are experiencing. Depressing yourself is a creative process, a form of self-realization. When you suspend all outer meanings as you do in depression, then *you* become the meaning. You achieve a greater inner clarity and create new inner meaning.

PAUL'S STORY

I left home Christmas Day for college. I couldn't stand being with my family one more day. When I got to college, no one was in the dorm, but it felt better to be alone and lonely than lonely and filled with my hatred toward my parents. The sadness I felt as I sat alone felt good to me.

Then Win showed up. Another depressed guy. Win was a compatriot. How nice it was to finally have someone who was as lonely and depressed as I was. It was exciting. I moved into his room to sleep, and he into mine to study. We slept during the day and talked and worked during the night. We bound ourselves together through our loneliness and depression.

Slowly the same forces that made me leave home began to make me want to leave my friend. I constantly chose not to talk when I didn't like something my friend did. I would rather sit alone and be depressed about it.

It worked against me in many ways. Emotionally he left me and I left him. We got into a terrible fight. I wanted him to stay my friend, and perhaps inside we still stayed friends. But outside nothing stayed the same.

I began to see the school psychiatrist who labeled me a manic depressive. What I remember most is walking into the psychiatrist's office, feeling broken-hearted and very desperate. I walked in and told the man that I wanted to kill myself. He looked removed and distant and told me, "So what, almost everyone wants to kill themselves." I knew right then that this man did not care about me either. That he could not talk to me. "So what . . ." I screamed inside as I sat there.

"So what . . ." I said to myself as I talked to myself for many months and years . . . because no one else could talk better to me. They labeled me and treated me with medication, but no one took the time to talk to me and really listen to my depression. And I didn't take the time for myself.

I finally met someone who would listen to my depression and talk to my depression. Someone who made more sense to me than did my own depression. He didn't say anything sometimes, but let me say all the depressing things I thought and felt; sometimes he said everything, and I could listen to something else other than my depression.

Paul was suspending the meanings he had learned in his family and trying to create new meanings. He was growing up.

There are many weaknesses in depression. Paul never had anyone to teach him the skill of perspective, to help him understand that his inner self had created the low self-image of his outer self as a way of helping him grow.

Paul became very strong in tearing down meanings, but he was a weakling in creating new ones. He began to think of himself as less than those around him, though all the time his inner self was getting stronger.

In the fitness approach it is critical that every time you depress an old activity or meaning you must replace it with a new meaning and activity. In this way you can bring your inner self and outer self into harmony.

Depression is an affirmation that you exist. During your depression you cut away all the nonsense of clichés, of style and fashion, and you see what is left. You realize, "Even amidst all these terrible and depressing thoughts I am alive. I am the reason."

As you move in the world, that is what becomes meaningful. Depression is taking a step to one side, away from the mainstream of your life. And from this oblique view you can decide if the path you are taking is the one you want. You become once again the chooser in your own life. Depression gives you the chance to develop a language and a personal philosophy which is meaningful to you.

SURVEY RESULTS ON DEPRESSION— A PLEASANT SURPRISE ▼

Throughout the surveys we have reported on a large group of fitness participants. We gave you these results so you could compare yourself in a general way to them. While many of them report frustration and worry and other problems, only 10 percent responded yes to the question about whether or not they were now depressed, while 95 percent responded that at some time during their life they had been depressed. It very well may be that when you allow yourself to become more active, you face new problems, but one problem you leave behind is depression.

Over 90 percent reported fatigue as a symptom of their depression, 78 percent reported tightness in body, and 58 percent reported numbness. These three physical characteristics are associated with holding in. The more you allow yourself to let go the less tired, the less tight you are, and the more feeling you have in your body.

What People Say

These are some comments we received from people who
labeled themselves as "seriously depressed" during some time
in their lives:

I fantasized a lot about becoming a star—also about
hanging myself. I never took either fantasy seriously.
I was mainly lonely and unhappy.   MARK

I believed I was alone [and had] to do everything by
myself. I tried to be proud of it. The more it didn't
work, the harder I tried. I took more and more tranquilizers to stop shaking and throwing up during the
day, more wine to go to sleep at night.   RICK

I would walk around like a robot and just go through
the motions of living. I believed that I was powerless
to help myself with anything. I gave up and had no
hope.   STEVEN

Gained thirty pounds in three months. Stayed away
from people my age. Felt very tired. Had difficulty
studying.   LISI

Stayed alone, didn't want to see anyone, only left my
apartment to go to work. I felt horrible, lay around,
watched TV waiting to feel better. Didn't care about
anything. Real lonely.   FRANK

I hated myself and contemplated life and suicide. I
wondered why everyone was insane.   PAUL

I was quiet and afraid to make contact with people.
I thought there was something very wrong with me
and everyone else. I had suspicious, hateful thoughts
about other people and myself. I would think a lot
about suicide and, when I grew older, of therapy.
                                    STEVE

HOW TO MAKE DEPRESSION
WORK FOR YOU

We disagree with the chemical approaches to depression currently used by some psychiatrists. We found that the opposite of depression is expression. What you are depressing is a strength. Depression makes you feel tired because it is so tiring holding in something powerful. Most people mislabel and abuse their strengths when often the real problem is that they have not yet developed the skills to make them work for them.

When working at a crisis center one of our colleagues received this suicide call:

PATIENT: Hello. Uh . . . I need some help. . . .

THERAPIST: What's the matter?

P: I'm depressed. Been depressed for two weeks. I want to kill myself.

T: What are you depressing?

P: What did you say?

T: What are you depressing?

P: You're crazy, didn't you hear me? I'm depressed and I want to kill myself!

T: Perhaps we have a bad phone connection. I said, what are you depressing?

P: (Pause) You mean that?

T: That is what I said.

P: I don't know what I am depressing.

T: Do you mean that?

P: I called for some comfort and counseling, and you are rude and not understanding.

T: Is that what you're depressing? That you need contact and understanding? I can understand that. I feel those same needs. I need people to talk to me, to help me work things out. It's too hard all alone.

P: Really? I thought I might be crazy.

T: I used to think that about myself, too. I want to know how you depress yourself.

P: What did you say? Did you say how do I depress myself?

T: Maybe we do have a bad connection.

P: No, I heard you. I don't know, except that I stop talking. My head goes a mile a minute.

T: You're talking now.

P: This doesn't count.

T: I count it.

P: Yeah, I count it, too.

As they talked the man who wanted to kill himself admitted he had strengths, but he didn't use them. He wound up thinking he wanted to kill himself only after trying to kill off his strengths in many little ways. Once he started admitting to his strengths and using them, he not only didn't want to kill himself, he felt better. As soon as he knew what he was depressing—wanting contact and understanding, both of which are positive psychological needs and potential strengths —he no longer felt hopeless. And then when he understood how he depressed himself, stopping talking and moving, both strengths that needed to be developed more, he had a direction in his life. Of course it was not a one-step cure. It took time for him to integrate what he had experienced in a way that undid his depression.

Nevertheless, it is important to remember that his depression was a test of his strengths. There is no test at once more difficult and easier to pass than a test we make up ourselves. We know what we know and what we don't know. He wanted to see if those strengths that he needed to develop more— talking, reaching out, and making contact—were stronger than all his negative and self-destructive thoughts. They were.

A Special Mind Jog for Severe Depression

One year, right around Christmas, we appeared on the "Good Morning America" show to talk about holiday depression. (National statistics do *not* indicate a higher incidence of hospitalization for depression at Christmas and New Year's. But people are more aware of the depression that already exists during the "season to be jolly.") The host asked, "What should a person do who feels really depressed and can't find anyone to talk to?" We gave him this mind jog: "When you are at the bottom of a depression and can't talk to anyone, actually start doing calisthenics to bring up your activity level. Begin doing jumping jacks and count aloud as you do them. Then get out of your room for a walk. Then go to a place where you will find people, even if you don't know them. Get your body in motion."

CONCLUSION

We understand both despair and depression as points for the beginning of psychological fitness. Life does not have to follow cycles of depression. Nor does prolonged depression guarantee that you are a deeper, more creative, more understanding human being. But your depression can help you know yourself.

As writers we can't resist giving you one last tip in changing your depression into a fitness technique. It is really easy. Just exchange the "d" for an "x," and mix it up, and you have expression. You can stop being depressed by beginning to express. You don't even have to understand it or like it; it is a fitness approach that works.

Phobias: Organized Fears versus Organized Living

A phobia is an irrational fear of some object, event, or situation, frequently involving compulsive rituals that seem ridiculous to an onlooker. But to the phobic person the rituals and the fears are deadly serious. Phobics frequently believe they will die if exposed to the situation they fear.

As strange as it may seem, the benefits of phobias are that they strengthen the connection between the inner self and outer self. When a person has a phobic reaction, he perceives something with his inner self, and he reacts to it in an exaggerated manner. In many ways the phobic is like a punch-drunk fighter who comes out flailing with his fists when there is no opponent.

The phobic reaction is an attempt to keep the inner self and outer self balanced. The inner self has developed strengths that the outer self is unable to use. In many ways a phobic is a psychological athlete who has overtrained one part of his body. He keeps building up this strength, and he never uses it in competition.

The phobic needs to regain perspective so that he can begin to channel all the psychological energy into new areas. We don't want the phobic to give up his behavior, we want him to expand his ability to use it in new areas of his life. If the phobic lost his intense and purposeful behavior, he would miss it. He would give up more than he gained. But when the phobic understands the strength his behavior can give him, he is free to find new behaviors that are more satisfying.

HOW PHOBIAS WORK

There are so many phobias that we could get lost asking why for each one. There is a different answer for each person. Phobias organize and focus our feelings and activities. A phobia is a way people contrive to *understand* their feelings when they lack the necessary strengths to have a natural understanding. This process is clear in the following story:

NUMBERS: JEAN'S STORY

My mother died on May 24, 1956, when I was nine years old. I have always remembered the afternoon that she died very vividly, even though for years I could not remember very much at all about the rest of my childhood. I think it was on the very night that she died that it first started. When I went to bed that night, I looked at the clock by my bedside and the only two numbers that I could really see were the 2 and the 4, 24, May 24.

As the days wore on, I started to become very afraid of those numbers. Somehow, I actually began to believe that if those two numbers were in my life at all, something awful would happen to me—maybe I would die, too. They became like a curse, and I tried to stay away from them at all costs. I began noticing 2's and 4's everywhere. It seemed like I couldn't get away from them.

I started trying very hard never to look at a clock in the afternoon. I was afraid that if I looked, I would see that it was either 2:20 or 4:10 (when the hands are on both the 2 and 4 at the same time). I started to really believe that if I would ever see a clock at exactly those times, some horrible catastrophe would befall me. In fact, as the years went by, I stopped looking at clocks and watches altogether, and never asked anyone what time it was (just to be safe). If I absolutely had to know what time it was, I looked with great fear, and kept something with me that had the number 3 on it. The number 3 had become my talisman, the magic number that would save me from some fate that I thought would be worse than death.

Every little daily event became fraught with the possibility of running into those numbers. For example, if I passed by my dad's desk in the den and noticed that there were two pencils sitting on top, I would have to quickly find another pencil somewhere to put with them so that there would be three pencils. Little things like this would happen every day.

I can remember the time my aunt gave me a ring for my birthday. When I opened the package, I became so panicked that I almost fainted. The ring had four birthstones on it! I tried very hard not to let anyone notice how frightened I was, but I was shaking so hard that to this day I'm sure my aunt had to have noticed. I remember making up a story about how the ring hurt my finger, and my aunt let me return it for another. I didn't like the ring that I traded for as much as the one my aunt picked for me, but it was the only one in my size that had three stones.

I lived this way for years, and never told anyone. I was just too afraid to say any of my thoughts out loud about the numbers. I know now that at nine years old, I was a very frightened and lonely little girl who developed a phobia to try in the only way I knew how to explain the engulfing fear I experienced when my mother left. Now, as an adult, I know it is no mystery why phobias develop, but I still feel sad when I think back and remember it all.

Jean organized her feelings around numbers. It could easily have been dogs or snakes or elevators. She was stopping her powerful feelings. Since she was unable to express and understand the feelings associated with the loss of her mother, she made up a new understanding. Her feelings remained powerful, but undeveloped.

It is important to understand that it was not her mother's death that caused her phobia. Jean was a girl with powerful feelings and she expressed them in the best way she could. She became so good at being a phobic and trying to feel her mother's loss that she continued this skill for years with all her feelings.

Most phobics find their phobias so unpleasant that they are relieved to learn a skill that rescues them from their own misunderstanding and frees them to enjoy *all* their misplaced feeling. Yet ironically the phobic needs the object of his phobia in order to continue his behavior. Without high places the acrophobic would have nothing to avoid. Some athletes develop positive phobias. They cling to a particular food, or sit under a pyramid, or swear by Wheaties. They are trying to make positive sense of their successes. But when things go wrong, they are quick to change socks, or switch from pyramids to copper bracelets, or check biorhythms.

These positive phobias are attempts at mind jogging. They don't work because the athlete has forgotten that it is not the particular ritual that makes him perform well, but the general fitness ritual of doing something and paying attention to the results.

Similarly, negative phobias are attempts to make sense of failures through ritualistic behavior. By the time a person has developed a phobia, he knows he is not performing as well as he wants. But he doesn't face his failure as a missing skill or weakness. Instead, he sees it as arising from some mysterious force.

A phobic is a mind jogger who doesn't know where the track is. His phobia is an incomplete skill. A positive behavior, repeated over and over, makes the phobic feel good. Because it is more intense than other parts of the phobic's life, his inner self refuses to give it up. It feels better to the inner self to be phobic and active than to be normal and passive.

When you understand phobias, you no longer fear them.

You learn how to strengthen them so they become assets to the personality.

MISCONCEPTIONS ABOUT PHOBIAS

Phobic people know something others don't. It is true that phobics sometimes become very well informed about their focus of fear. For example, some aerophobics know all about airline crashes, but are unconvinced by the fact that every passenger who flies has a 99.999 percent chance of surviving. They act as though their fear gives them special knowledge beyond the facts.

Phobias are inexplicable and mysterious. Not true. Most phobics can relate scary incidents that triggered their phobia. They know the relevant events in their personal history, but this knowledge alone doesn't change their irrational fear.

Phobics can be cured by the sink or swim method. Some phobics do successfully endure total immersion in the feared situation, but their phobia doesn't automatically disappear. Gradual change is much better.

People will just outgrow their phobias. Phobias can persist for decades. Unless the phobic person effectively tries to change, he will most likely continue to be phobic. Worse than that, he will start to be afraid of showing the phobia, and then he has a double phobia—the phobic fear and his fear of the phobia.

Phobias are fascinating. Some phobics do act as though everyone should be interested in their fears. But phobias are basically very boring because they are narrowing. Without the phobia, the phobic opens up to a wide range of emotions.

Getting over phobias is terribly painful and difficult. At Synanon, addicts who go off drugs totally report that it is about as painful as a bad cold or flu, no more and no less. It's the same with breaking a phobia—you will feel a lot, but your feelings won't kill you. They are about as intense as a roller coaster ride.

THE HIDDEN STRENGTH OF PHOBIAS

The phobic has a tremendous ability to plan and organize but ends up over-focused and over-organized. He attempts to understand and plan his life to the point that it no longer makes sense to those around him—or to himself either.

KNIVES: JACK'S STORY

When I was twenty-two years old I spent about a half hour every night before going to bed hiding all the knives in the house from myself. Why would I do such a bizarre thing? Well, because for about two years, I honestly believed that if I didn't, I would kill someone in the middle of the night while I was asleep.

During the day I knew that what I was doing every night was irrational, even "crazy." I would tell myself how unreal my fear was, and promise myself that "tonight I won't do such a silly thing." But when bedtime approached, I would get the same very sickening feeling in my stomach, and my thoughts would begin racing —"But what if while you're asleep, when you have no control over your impulses, you sleepwalk into the kitchen, pick up a knife, and go stab someone?"

I believed that while asleep I'd lose the conscious control over myself and my impulses. Against all my rational knowledge that what I was doing every night was, to say the least, unusual, I felt compelled to hide the knives one more time. I'd walk into the kitchen and take all the knives and sharp objects like scissors and ice picks and put them in the back of the dishwasher—then I'd place a lot of dishes and glasses in front of them, lock the dishwasher door, shut the door to the kitchen, lock that, and then place a chair in front of the door. My reasoning was that if I had to go through all those steps to get to the knives, it would surely wake me up—and then, once awake, I'd have control over myself again.

I felt ashamed of my behavior, and was afraid to tell anyone what I was doing. I tried very hard (and succeeded) to look and act perfectly normal to my friends and family—but the pressure of my phobic behavior became so great and frightened me so much that after

a year and a half I sought professional help. Today, what
at one time seemed like such a complicated, unfathom-
able "emotional illness" has just become a bad memory.

Undeveloped Strengths

All of the phobic's other skills become subservient to the
organizing around the phobia. Feeling is undeveloped because
it is directed at the phobia. Activity is undeveloped because
it is directed at the phobia and away from making contact.
The phobic needs help in developing the skills of making
contact. With these, the phobia will disappear because the
person is focusing on his life.

The weakness in a phobia is that, eventually, the phobic becomes so engrossed in developing this single strength that he
stops using any other strength that he has. Other areas of his
personality begin to atrophy. He sets up a cycle that will
eventually entrap him. Though using his strength feels good to
his inner self, it also wants the development of all the potential
strengths. So the inner self begins attacking the phobic behavior by turning the focus away from an object (such as
snakes) to the person himself. He then begins to fear himself
and what he does as much as he once did an outside object.
The inner self will settle for nothing less. It wants to break
the limiting behavior. It needs to expand. If this means attacking what it once promoted it will do so.

We try to teach phobics to stop punishing themselves and
begin using the fitness perspective. A phobia is a way of giving ourselves attention. We give ourselves attention by focusing our outer behavior on an inner perception or feeling.
When a phobic can begin identifying this basic process—
focusing on his inner self—he is no longer trapped. He has
discovered his basic strength. If he begins mind jogging, he
will acquire the skills he needs to use that strength to make
himself a more effective and fit human being.

SURVEY RESULTS FOR PHOBIAS ▼

Authorities estimate there are about thirty million phobics who need help or have sought treatment. In a survey we conducted with 250 people who participated in a Psychological Fitness Program, 79 percent reported that they had at one time suffered from phobias. Of these, 34 percent said that they were bothered by their phobias daily. When asked if they still experienced phobic feelings in the present, 59 percent responded affirmatively and 29 percent of those said that these experiences occurred daily.

The most frequent physical symptoms associated with the onset of the phobia were increased pulse (reported by 89 percent of the people), pounding heart (84 percent), perspiration (57 percent), and physical immobility (53 percent).

Social phobias (fear of meeting people) were reported most often (21 percent), with animal phobias reported next (12 percent), and fear of sex, fear of heights, and fear of closed spaces all were reported by 9 percent. Many people (73 percent) reported suffering from more than one phobia at the same time.

What People Say about Phobias

If we leave the labels behind, here are some views of people who have suffered from phobias:

I would think about being killed all the time and I would be scared to go anywhere and when I did I would be very tense and get migraine headaches.

DANA

When I was in high school I had a bad drug experience. I had a panic attack and thought I was going to die. For months after that I would experience the

same feeling when I was alone in crowds so I avoided
them (i.e., the high school cafeteria, etc.)

LAURIE

I couldn't go to sleep because I thought I would die.

JEAN

I was sure someone was in the closet and was going
to kill me. I'd feel so scared I wouldn't talk or make
any sound, and I'd *never* turn my back to the closet.

GARY

Fear I wouldn't be able to breathe after I went to
sleep, or I'd stop breathing before I went to sleep.
Would blow my nose, take Vicks, put water in my
nose, etc., every night for several months.

ROSE

I thought I had a heart condition. I constantly listened
to my heartbeat. I never believed doctors when they
said I had a good, healthy heart.   JACK

When I went near someone who was deformed or had
a disease I would hold my breath so as not to breathe
the same air as the person and keep from getting sick.

FRANK

I had a phobia about having dirty or grimy-feeling
hands. I would wash my hands often and be afraid of
getting germs on them.   ALAN

I have always been terrified of heights. I panic and
become physically immobilized when on something
higher than four feet.   JEAN

I had phobias of heights. I would fantasize myself
falling, then being crushed, and dying when I hit the
ground. I would get a rush in my entire body, and my
sense of balance would be distorted.   STEVE

I had thought devils could get me. Scared of possession, dogs, the dark, devils in the dark, bad men in the closet.   KATHY

I was afraid of frogs. My father said I would have terrible warts and blisters on my hands if I played with frogs.   ROBERT

For about two years I had terrifying nightmares about snakes and rats. I believed they were in my room, hidden in the woodwork or under the bed. I would run down the hall and try to jump on the bed without letting my feet touch the floor of the bedroom. I'd cover my head with the sheet to try and keep them out; I'd lie awake for a long time fearing the slightest press or movement of the sheet for fear they were crawling on top of me. I'd fall asleep and dream they were crawling over me and wake up screaming.

BARBARA

I used to be terrified of spiders. I'd be so scared I would worry a lot of the time even when I didn't see one, that one would see me. I used to be able to figure out when it was time to see one—when one would come into my room.   KATHY

After being discharged from the hospital I had a phobia of smelling ether or even thinking of it. I became dizzy and anxious. Also, if I heard a motor, I felt anxious (a motor like a respirator). I had anxiety attacks for years.   RON

CONCLUSION

Phobias are actually indirect ways of paying attention to yourself when you don't have the skills to do it directly. Here are two simple mind jogs that you can try to begin helping you discover that you are focusing on yourself.

Two Special Mind Jogs for Phobias

Mind Jog One. Begin to pair up your favorite food with thoughts and images of what you fear. For example, if you like ice cream and are afraid of cars, start to think of cars in ice cream colors. "That's a strawberry Cadillac," "That's a lemon sherbet Chevy," "That's a chocolate Porsche." Spend an entire day labeling cars this way. Then sit in a car. Then, eat an ice cream cone while the car is running but not moving. Finally, go for a ride, but don't ride any longer than your ice cream lasts. You will be conditioning yourself by pairing something you like with something you fear. If you like ice cream enough, you will start to overcome your fear.

Mind Jog Two. Choose a phobia partner. He can be a spouse or a good friend. Whenever you begin to notice the old familiar fear beginning to grab on to you, try to contact your partner. Talk about *any other feeling* that you had that day. Keep a little record of the effects of this jog.

If there was a special pill that we had discovered that would take away your phobia, we wouldn't give it to you. Your phobia filled a need. We want you to use it as a way of finding your fitness identity. We want your inner self to experience the fear or sadness within the phobic situation so that your inner self will teach your outer self how to begin living with more feeling. It will strengthen your entire personality.

Whenever we interviewed people who have gotten over phobias on their own, we almost always got the same answer to the question, "How did you do it?" People say, "I just had to do it, so I did." Often this answer comes from people who had narrowed their lives severely to avoid work, play, or social situations in which they might confront the thing they feared.

And then, suddenly, something came along that they wanted more than their fear, and the phobia was confronted and conquered. Once the phobic person makes the decision to do something despite his fears he is able to mobilize his strengths. He can use his focusing and organizing skills to plan the new activities with as much attention and involvement as he usually gave to his planned avoidances. When he does that, an expansion occurs that shifts the sensations from fear to excitement.

From Weighing to Wanting

Weight problems have little to do with eating. People have weight problems because they are stuck with the personality dynamics involved in gaining and losing weight. Gaining weight feels good, and losing weight feels good. During the gaining phase the outer self is given free rein to do what it wants, and then during the losing phase the inner self takes control. There is no such thing as being an out-of-control eater. Gaining and losing weight is the psychological exercise of strengthening the outer self and then the inner self.

The person with weight problems is actually suffering from a communication problem between his inner self and outer self, which are fighting each other instead of working together. Each is like a separate personality that thinks he will not get to develop his strength if the other is around.

When a person has this conflict, the inner self wants a greater say and control, while the outer self wants more freedom and independence. These goals are not contradictory. If, in fact, a person allows himself to bring these two selves together, he will have everything that he wants—psychological fitness.

While you are dieting you are moving closer and closer to connecting your inner self and outer self. Since you don't have all the personality skills you need to maintain that connection you gain the weight back so you can start all over again.

People overeat and diet as a form of psychological exercise. Everyone who has ever lost weight knows that losing weight is not that hard in and of itself. It actually feels good. You have a purpose and direction. What is ineffective about dieting is that it is repetitive. When you begin to use the psychological fitness perspective to understand the personality dynamics of your dieting you will find it much easier to lose weight. You will have less desire to gain weight back because you will be using that same personality exercise in new areas of your life.

Remember, you are trying to find an identity which is as dynamic as you feel when you are dieting, an identity that focuses the same intensity, direction, and purpose you put into your dieting, but without the problem of being fat. Psychological fitness doesn't solve particular problems. It reveals to you your dynamic sense of identity.

THE HOW OF WEIGHT

Until you take the time to understand how a person behaves, no diet will work over a long period of time. Being overweight is just like any other psychological problem. It is an attempt at a solution. It just happens to be a solution that makes you gain weight.

People gain weight because they want, not food or drink, but their own wanting. A diet that only tells you what to eat leaves your wanting unsatisfied.

Your inner self knows this. But your outer self tries to convince your inner self that what you want is food. If you took the time to ask yourself if you really wanted to eat that particular food, you would more times than not answer no.

The how of weight is wanting. The more that you allow yourself to express your own wanting, to share it, to have wanting feasts, the more time you will spend mind jogging and the less time eating. It is hard to admit, but eating never satisfies your wanting. Only giving your inner self what it wants—wanting—will fill you up.

MISCONCEPTIONS ABOUT WEIGHT

There are many good "reasons" for letting your body be some way other than how you want it.

Being fat (or skinny) is . . . my natural state, my bone structure, the way I was born. While there are cases of real physiological problems, imagined problems are often used as excuses. People who are noticeably over- or underweight have lost the connection between their inner and outer selves. They need to practice hearing and seeing skills so that they can begin to identify their real body image.

Fat people are happy being that way. There is a myth that heavy people are jolly and gregarious. Their concern with food and diets reflects the often unstated dissatisfaction with which they live. This dissatisfaction is one of the major strengths of people with weight problems. It can be used to start them changing their feelings about their bodies.

There is nothing wrong with being fat. Any good doctor will tell you to diet if he feels that you are overweight. Too many pounds also weigh on you psychologically.

THE HIDDEN STRENGTH OF BEING OVERWEIGHT

The hidden strength beneath the fat is the wanting. Fat people have not diversified their wanting into all the areas of their life. When a person eats too much, he has turned all his wanting into eating. He becomes focused on a very narrow range of feeling. "I want to eat" has substituted for "I want friends," "I want contact," "I want to play," "I want to look good." The more eating substitutes for wanting, the fatter the person becomes. It is directly proportional.

The overweight person is like the phobic in reverse. Instead of trying to avoid something, he feels compelled to consume it. Food becomes the focus of all that is good or bad in his life. Diet books outsell other popular books, year after year, because people are always seeking answers. They get confused because they are told that to lose weight they have to oppose their greatest strength—wanting to eat.

Eventually they are so confused that they are not even sure whether being fat is good or bad. They get mixed up about their own body image.

Body Image: A Person's Self-Awareness

Your body image is your awareness of how you feel inside —how you feel *in your body.*

The overweight person cannot clearly differentiate between what feels right on the inside and how he looks on the outside. He has substituted eating for feelings for so long that what is happening on the inside becomes obscure.

FAT BEAUTY: BETTY

I grew up with a mother who made me feel fat and ugly. She told me I wore a size "16" in clothes, never showed me how to fix my hair, always bought my clothes on sale, rarely took much interest in me. Most of the time I think I was an afterthought with her.

I grew up believing I was a "big" girl who was plain and wore thick glasses. Just like the neglect I felt inside, I hated how I looked. I was too fat, unfashionable, and unattractive to men. Nothing I did could cure that hollowness and loneliness inside me.

I became obsessed with my weight. All I thought about was if only I were thin then I would finally "be popular" and have friends and not be so miserable. Un-

fortunately, nothing seemed to work. I "dieted" all the
time, yet always remained twenty pounds overweight.
I spent hours sewing dresses that never looked good
once they were finished. They were tailored perfectly,
but the style was hopelessly out of vogue. I would go to
bed at night in painfully prickly rollers in the hope of
looking beautiful, yet I couldn't seem to create a hair-
style that made me look pretty.

I always felt my main weakness in life was being overweight and unattractive.

The overweight person often thinks he is bad when he
feels bad. This feeling represents the discrepancy between the
way he is on the outside (body appearance) and the way he
feels on the inside (body awareness). When body appearance
and body awareness come together, the body image is back
in focus. It takes more than a diet to accomplish this, as we
will show.

SOME FAT FACTS AND BODY IMAGE
SURVEY RESULTS ▼

Research on the relationship between weight, drugs,
and socioeconomic status has revealed many fascinating trends. For example, 88 percent of the legitimate
use of amphetamines is for the short-term control of
obesity. It is a form of legalized drug addiction.

Weight has a lot to with social class and the images
associated with it. Women at higher income levels
were 20 percent leaner and their husbands were 20
percent fatter than their counterparts in lower income
brackets. Women who didn't go to high school were
generally 33 percent fatter than women with twelve
years or more of education. Men with a college education were 10 percent fatter than those with no high
school education.

We asked over 250 participants in our fitness programs whether they were satisfied with their body
image. We included weight, height, and shape. Males
reported 54 percent yes and females 52 percent yes.
Over 70 percent of both sexes reported at some period
in their life that they focused excessively and nega-
tively on their body image—a focus which lasted for
years.

The parts of their bodies they most liked and disliked were:

Liked	Disliked
height	weight
eyes	muscle tone
ears	chest
face	stomach
neck	*thighs

* Thighs were the only area in which sex was a sig-
nificant factor in the response—64 percent of the
women disliked their thighs to 25 percent of the men.

What is most interesting is this survey is not about
being fat or skinny, but about body image.

What People Say about Their Body Images

The survey data are reflected in what these people told us
about their bodies:

> Starting about age fourteen I hated parts of my body
> and how unproportionate my body is. Small top/large
> bottom. Thought about it every day. Wanted to cut
> parts of bottom and put onto top.
>
> **NANCY**

> I wanted to have a really strong, powerful body. Later
> I was always a little overweight, and I worried about
> it *all* the time. I felt disgusted with myself.
>
> **JEFF**

In high school, I thought that my legs were too long, my arms too long, and my torso too short. I was so depressed about it, I considered suicide.

SCOTT

I was in the Navy. I was a fanatic about exercising and lifting weights. I worried about how I looked all the time.   TOM

I had lost a lot of weight, then I gained it back and more. I hated myself all the time and how I looked. I never wanted to see anyone.   ELAINE

I focused on the shape of my body, my stomach, tits, nothing was right, there was something wrong with everything.   WENDY

I hated my body—I wanted to change myself—I thought I was ugly to women—I had the shape of my nose changed.   VINCENT

I used to *hate* my legs and my stomach. I would always look at other girls' legs and compare them to mine—that would be the first thing I'd look at—I would hate myself and fantasize about having an operation to change how I looked.   NANCY

I thought my thighs were too fat, and I hated starting to get breasts. I thought my nose was too big, and I hated my complexion. I felt self-conscious all the time, and I started to hide my breasts with my hands and clothes. I was always putting my hand over my nose. I would dream about having a clean complexion. I felt awkward and ugly and couldn't talk.

LINDA

Feeling very heavy and fat; feeling like I had a nice face and the rest of me could be passable. Always feeling like I had to cover my body.   GALE

I've never enjoyed my large breasts; I've been afraid men were "only after" my body; I've been fat for many years.   SHEILA

THE SECRET TO LOSING WEIGHT

The secret to losing weight is to develop other personality and life strengths for, if you are too weak in other areas to change your lifetime eating pattern, you are trapped forever into being fat. No matter how many times you lose weight, *unless you have developed other strengths that give you as much pleasure as eating you cannot maintain a slimmer body weight and appearance.*

CAROLE'S STORY

I used to be fixated on food and cooking. I woke up in the morning thinking about my first meal and spent hours cooking up great breakfasts, lunches, and dinners. I subscribed to cooking magazines and cut out their best recipes. I spent more energy around food-related activities than anyone else.

I felt bad most of my life because I was fat and felt unattractive. I felt ashamed of my cravings for food. I acted like a wallflower and cringed every time I had to undress around anyone—especially a man. I felt trapped in twenty layers of fat and couldn't escape. One of my daily fantasies was cutting off the extra fat on my thighs and stomach with a large butcher knife. Secretly my greatest wish was to be thin, pretty, and popular.

That wish never materialized until my late twenties. I lost weight and learned how to change my "food energy" to other avenues of pleasure. When I felt the urge to stuff my mouth, I learned that my body was wanting something very strongly and that I just didn't know the skills of getting those other things.

I discovered sports. Having been unathletic most of my adult life, this didn't come easy at first, but I tried. Instead of cooking, eating, and reading recipes I learned to run—to spring and to sweat. I learned stretching my body and yoga.

I was taught volleyball and basketball and baseball. Amazingly, I felt more. Instead of being tired, bored, and lethargic a lot of the time, I began to feel physically tired after working out and relaxed in a new way.

Other things changed, also. Instead of being the "house cook," I got other people to help me, and I started eating out in restaurants more. I ordered foreign foods and different appetizers instead of salad-meat-potato meals. I learned to "dominate" the conversation at dinner time instead of feeling dominated by the food on my plate. I dropped my subscriptions to the food magazines and started creating my own original dishes.

I still am food-oriented, but not a slave to my appetite. I feel much more balanced in my life and more like a human being. Sure, the urges to overeat and drift off into my "food world" are still there, but they don't control me and make me miserable. I feel like I have found a way out of a twenty-year nightmare. I have learned to love myself.

The Psychological Fitness Diet

The first step to the fitness diet is to find out what your real inner opinion of yourself is. Most people admit that deep down they have a good opinion of themselves though it may be covered over with problems and negative thoughts which occupy most of the day. But way inside there is not the image of the fat man or the fat woman, but of a person who looks and feels good.

You need to develop that image. As you admit openly what your inner image is, you will begin naturally to develop the strengths that you need in order to become that way.

You must concentrate on what you want to do rather than on what you don't want to do. Your eating will decrease because you will want to save room for other things in your life that give you pleasure. Your psychological fitness will expand as your waistline naturally decreases.

What and How to Eat

What you need to eat is a sensible and balanced diet. The main characteristic of the diet is movement. Being physically active means, for many men and women, changing their outer image of themselves as nonphysical. The key to dieting is time. Diet for a lifetime. Diet so that your entire eating changes. Change the meaning of diet to choice of foods rather than the decision not to eat.

Two Special Mind Jogs for the Overweight

Mind Jog One. Think about everything that excites you besides eating—shopping for new clothes, painting, watching television, skiing, listening to music, whatever. Make a list and rank in order of preference. Now, for five days, do one thing from your list. Think about that activity replacing some of your food-thinking energy. Be aware of the level of excitement you experience doing your new activity. You are learning a new way to make yourself happy.

Mind Jog Two. Here's what to do when all you want to do is stuff food in your mouth.

   a.   First, lie down by yourself for at least five minutes. Breathe nice and slow. Become aware of your chest, your arms, legs, stomach, and head. Do you feel panicked? Tense? Irritable? Stirred up inside? Bored? Does your head ache? Is your stomach tight? Slow down enough so you at least have some awareness of sensation inside your body. Sing a song to yourself or hum a tune . . . make a little noise.

   b.   Now, go back to your food and take one big bite of something good—something you really want, not just anything to stuff in your mouth.

   c.   Step in front of a mirror. This will be hard, but look closely at your body. The chances are it will be hard for you to do this, but do it anyway. Just look and be aware, inside, of how you feel. Is it hard to see parts of your body? Do you want to look away? Do you feel something in the pit of your stomach?

d. Now, go back and take another bite of something—again, something good.

e. Next, try with all your might to leave the kitchen and walk around the block. Take your time and look at the different houses and the people inside and what they are doing. Think about the people (if any) in your house and people that you know. Think about how you are feeling at that moment . . . if you are still restless, bored, lonely, or whatever. If you are near a store, stop in and buy yourself something nonedible—something you wouldn't ordinarily buy, something nice.

f.   Finally, if you still want to eat some more, go to a restaurant or a friend's house and eat something . . . in public.

What these mind jogs are trying to do is break your "food syndrome" of putting food into your mouth *without noticing how* you feel inside. They are exercises in rechanneling your energy into something more satisfying.

CONCLUSION

The hidden strength of the overweight person is his wanting. The not-so-hidden weakness is that he too narrowly focuses his wanting on food. Once that wanting is freed and redirected it becomes a powerful force for psychological fitness.

19

Tension and Anxiety

Many people don't want to know what tension does for them. They want to remove it by taking two aspirin, or a double scotch, or Valium three times a day. No matter what you take—tension exists for everyone. When used constructively tension is the energy of life. It can help you build the psychological strengths that you need to fulfill your potential.

If you lack the skills to release your tension, then you begin to identify yourself as anxious or nervous. What is really occurring is that your inner self and your outer self are temporarily disconnected. As you use tension for your psychological fitness you discover the very active process of relaxation. People make themselves tense because they like the way it feels and they like what they can do with it. What we are going to teach you is a way of using tension so that you learn to alternate it with relaxation.

When a person is out of touch with his need for tension he will often experience anxiety. The person will report a nervousness and a body uneasiness. He has lost contact with his inner self. He will say that he feels tense because of a certain situation or person, but he is sadly mistaken. It is his inner self making him tense, as a message for his outer self. He is preparing his body to perform at its peak.

THE HOW OF TENSION

If you can learn to release your tension directly, then you will relax. Tensing is a building up of responses. If those responses are all held in, they become tension or anxiety. If they are released they become action. Tensing is a natural way of strengthening the personality, but it must be accompanied by releasing if the strength is going to be used.

Releasing yourself psychologically is what makes the personality integrate the strengths that it has been developing. The more you are able to release the more you are able to use your tension to make yourself feel better. If you cannot release tension, then you are left always at the ready unable to give yourself the "at ease" command.

MISCONCEPTIONS ABOUT TENSION

Avoid the things that make you tense. If you try to avoid things that make you anxious you can end up avoiding almost anything and everything—dogs, cats, people, stairways, sunshine, dark streets, working, not working, restaurants, eating alone, etc. Don't avoid anxiety-provoking situations, avoid doing what you usually do in those situations. Change your behavior not your environment, otherwise general anxieties become specific phobias.

Tension is a signal of an impending nervous breakdown. If this were true, we would all be in a lot of trouble! Tension or anxiety is a signal that you are feeling something and not doing and expressing enough about your feeling.

Tension should be medicated. If your heart is racing, run the race, don't try to medicate your heartbeat. Many people believe this misconception to such an extent that their greatest anxiety is running out of tranquilizers.

Only weak people get anxious. People who overlook the signals from their sympathetic nervous system are suffering from psychic anesthesia. Anxiety is not a signal that you will fail at what you want to do, it is a sign that what you do matters to you.

Anxiety attacks are predictable and uncontrollable. You can't control *when* you will feel something or be anxious, but you can control *how* you will be anxious.

THE HIDDEN STRENGTHS
AND WEAKNESSES OF TENSION

The hidden strength of tension is that it prepares you to handle crises and emergencies. The more you use tension the less you perceive it as a threat. People who experience chronic tension are actually out of touch with themselves—their outer selves are unrelated to their inner selves. When the inner self and outer self are synchronized, you can use the outer tension to get ahead and for creative work, while at the same time being relaxed about the way you go about getting what you want. The more intelligently you use the interplay between the inner and outer selves the more willing you are to use tension to your advantage.

When your inner self and outer self are not synchronized, you begin to experience chronic tension, because you don't know how to release it.

David was a good example of someone who learned to use tension. When he first started in our programs, every time he had something to say he would get tense because he knew he would stutter.

STUTTERING: DAVID'S STORY

I have stuttered ever since I began talking. I have had negative thoughts about myself ever since I can remember. I am never sure which came first. What I remember clearly is that, for most of my life, I felt bad. And since I also stuttered, I naturally felt bad when I stuttered.

Somewhere I got the idea my stuttering was bad. Whenever I had something to say I became anxious. I knew I would stutter. And I knew I would feel bad about myself.

When I began the program I began hearing things about myself that I had never heard before. All that I knew was that it was hard to hear positive things said to me. For years as a child I was used to hearing the opposite.

"If only I didn't stutter, if only I didn't stutter," I would cry. Now I was being told my stuttering was something good, something positive, something powerful. I could hardly believe it. It didn't fit with my old beliefs.

I learned that stuttering meant feeling explosions—having more feeling than I do words.

David learned how to enjoy his stuttering. Tension for him meant he was getting excited. He sometimes just needed to release. And if that meant stuttering he would stutter. The more that David learned what his tension meant and how he could release the tension by allowing himself to stutter, the better he felt about himself and the less he stuttered. Though he still stutters sometimes, it doesn't mean he has to be tense when he is stuttering.

As you learn to use your tension you begin learning when and how to relax. Mostly you have to stop tightening yourself, getting yourself ready, when in fact you want to stop and relax.

ANXIETY SURVEY RESULTS ▼

Asked how often they experience anxiety, 43 percent of those asked said several times a day and 23 percent said daily. Of those surveyed, 80 percent at some period in their life experienced excessive anxiety, and 41 percent said that anxiety lasted years. Thirty-two percent now experience excessive anxiety.

The number one physical symptom reported for anxiety was tightness in body; number two was fidgetiness; number three, fatigue; number four, poor coordination; number five, aches and pains; and number six, headaches.

What People Say about Anxiety

I would become so anxious that I could take three Thorazine and drink a six-pack of tall beers before I would become *reasonably* nervous. I would have periods where I would be so afraid that I refused to go out of the house and wouldn't get out of bed. If I was out with friends at a restaurant, I would have to go to the bathroom by myself to try to calm down because I'd be shaking, and I was afraid everyone would see.   VICKI

I always worried about what was wrong—I didn't "feel there." I was in my own little world. I was lonely being so anxious all the time. I didn't know why I was or what to do or even that I was. I was almost always that way.   BETTY

I was constantly in a state of worrying, feeling tense, nervous feeling in my stomach, unable to sleep well, feeling fidgety, ringing in my ears.   SHERRY

I'd be very scared about big horrors—my father dying, or my brother being drafted—and at times couldn't sleep for hours thinking of things like that.

BOB

I constantly worried about where my life was going. I was unable to focus or sleep.   JAMES

I was always afraid; afraid of the worst happening, and I felt out of control, small and weak, and unable to change things or make them better.   MIKE

I was constantly afraid; afraid if someone knocked on the door or if the phone rang. Much of the time I wouldn't answer my door or phone. I would literally hide in my house with most of the lights out so no one would know I was home.   FRANK

I couldn't make the simplest decision. Taking my truck in for a lube seemed totally overwhelming.

DICK

Here is the story of one person who was able to learn how to use tension and stress in a new way:

THE ANIMAL DOCTOR

I wanted to be a veterinarian since I was twelve years old. In one way or another, every day at school revolved around the day that I'd walk up to the podium to accept my DVM degree.

I had one major drawback though—I was weak in math—but I figured if I worked twice as hard as the smarter students, I might make it. So throughout both high school and college I did nothing but study—I never dated or went to parties. I didn't always make A's, but what I lacked in academic ability I made up in the sheer number of hours that I studied. Finally I was accepted to Vet School and I should have been elated—but I wasn't. I saw it as just another hurdle to get over and another bunch of students to compete against. Again, if

I studied twice as hard as my classmates I could keep my head above water, and for four grueling years I treaded water like hell—constantly striving for the one thing that had any meaning to me—getting that degree.

In 1975 I was made a Doctor of Veterinary Medicine. After fifteen years of studying I had made it . . . and again I should have been elated, but I wasn't. Instead I felt lost. I tried to get a practice going, but something went wrong with every effort I made—the wrong people, the wrong location, financial problems. For two years one stress followed another.

I'd achieved my goal of fifteen years, but something was very wrong in my life. I had everything I needed (I thought) to finally get my career started, but nothing would start. I'd come face to face with myself, and I felt nervous and anxious constantly.

When I began the psychological fitness program I found out what was wrong. I found out that I had been taught to study and how to work under stress and pressure, but I'd never been taught to *value* any of my strengths that got me through all those years. I learned that I had a lot of determination, that I was willing to work hard for something I wanted—things I have never been taught to give myself credit for. I was also taught how to use these strengths in the other parts of my life that I'd neglected for so long—to make friends, or to just have fun. I learned that there was more to life than winning the war. For the first time in my life I was taught how to appreciate winning all the little battles along the way.

USING YOUR HIDDEN STRENGTH

The key to discovering and using the hidden strengths behind anxiety is to focus on *how* you are anxious and not *what* you are anxious about. The next time you feel very anxious notice how you are. Say to yourself:

"I'm *being* anxious in *this* way."

Don't say to yourself, "I'm having an anxiety attack" or "I'm too anxious to function."

Once you begin to observe yourself being anxious you will notice that you do not use your full personality. You will see that you do not match the increase in your feeling level with an increase in expression and activity. Once you do, then anxiety more and more becomes excitement and anticipation and alertness rather than worry and dread and the jitters.

The Fitness Perspective on Anxiety

Anxiety and unresolved tension can lead, over a long period of time, to hypertension. But when you know how to use the fitness approach you can change these potentially deadly weaknesess into powerful strengths. When most people feel tense or anxious they turn away from themselves. They try to stop the anxiety by getting away from what is producing it. In the fitness perspective we teach people to face it. Relaxing can give you a new perspective on how you want to be, and getting away gives you a break; but both of these techniques limit your behavior. To be fully fit you must be able to face your anxiety and conquer it so that it becomes a source, in and of itself, of dynamic and active relaxation. When you learn to be relaxed while active you are performing up to your maximum.

Tensing is necessary if you want to get a peak performance from yourself. By mind jogging your tension you will turn it into tensing. When you begin to get anxious or tense in any situation, you can begin a new dialogue between your inner and outer selves. You can realize that you are tense—and then can evaluate whether you are really preparing for something or have just fallen into a habit. If you are preparing for something, then use the tensing to improve your performance— but if the tension is just outmoded habit, then you can begin using your new psychological fitness skills to release it.

Afterword
Fitness for Your Lifetime

The fitness approach to most psychological problems (such as phobias, tension, and depression) is that they signal a need to grow and develop. But there is a need for fitness exercises even when no special problems exist. Psychological fitness is mainly for people who are doing O.K. in their lives but want more—people who want the best for themselves and from themselves. Psychological fitness is for people who want to live at a peak level of feeling, awareness, and activity.

The game of life is not mastered in youth, middle age, or old age. You must keep playing as you grow older. A lifetime of psychological fitness depends on a lifetime of mind jogging. As Frank Lloyd Wright said, "The longer I live the more beautiful life becomes."

THE MANY STAGES OF LIFE

Children are not the only people who go through stages. Simply growing older requires psychological growth. Psychological characteristics that were strengths at one age become weaknesses at a later age. Consider the story of Billy J.:

BILLY: INNOCENCE PROLONGED

Billy J. was twenty-five but looked like a teenager and acted like one. When Billy was in high school it had been the best time of his life. He played on the basketball and football teams. He dated the rally girls and belonged to the best men's club on campus. But Billy J. wasn't good enough to play college sports and he didn't really want to attend college anyway.

From age nineteen to age twenty-five Billy J. had held fifteen different jobs. He was likable and could get hired easily, but he couldn't hold a job. The problem was that Billy thought jobs were like classes. He believed he could cut work days just as he had often cut classes.

The charming adventuresome devil-may-care spirit that had made Billy J. popular in high school made him a loser as a worker. He had not developed new strengths to change old weaknesses.

Billy's personality profile went from a "high" in school to a "low" as a young adult. His personality dynamics were being used inefficiently and, as a result, conflicts developed between his inner self and outer self. This conflict led to his unfit behavior. His lifetime of fitness had ended by the time he was seventeen or eighteen.

According to the theories of Erik Erikson, Billy J. could be described as someone who had not yet successfully passed through the basic crisis of adolescence—finding his own identity. Billy J. was stuck in a confusion of roles; he was neither a young adult nor a kid.

GROWING VS. AGING

Some authorities have argued that middle age, that period from age thirty on, lasts forty to forty-five years. That's a long time. Most people believe that they are grown up by age thirty, but recent evidence suggests that everyone can have a long, long middle period of growth.

GROWING WITH AGE

Dr. Joanne Stevenson, an associate professor of nursing at Ohio State University, has observed that "although some middle agers experience physical decline they continue to grow emotionally and intellectually well into their seventies."

In a series of research studies conducted by Dr. Robert Havighurst and his colleagues at the University of Chicago, it was found that older people who remained actively engaged in life were generally healthier and happier than those who withdrew from social contacts.

It is vitally important for people to set up active lifestyles in their middle years because patterns of aging are predictable from middle age. People who are psychologically slowing down in their forties and fifties are likely to be stalled by their sixties and seventies. But even stalls can be restarted:

DECIDING TO GROW: A CASE EXAMPLE

The oldest person to participate in our psychological fitness program was sixty-five. She was dying from cancer but traveled three thousand miles from her home on the East Coast to spend a month in Los Angeles. She had been widowed for ten years and had stopped dating after five years. During the fitness program she became aware that she still very much wanted a good relationship with a man. But she believed she couldn't really date someone because of her short life expectancy. We convinced her to try.

What she discovered was that her intense awareness of death made for an intense awareness of life and living. Her relationships deepened much faster than before— there was nothing to hold back and nothing to wait for. Within a month she began to date one man steadily,

and soon their relationship was as close as though they
had lived together for a decade.

You have a choice: grow or just age. People who continue
to develop their personality by extending strengths and developing weaknesses into strengths never stop growing. They
are always ready for something new.

CHECK IN WITH YOURSELF

In the psychological fitness approach you check in with
yourself. You check what you know best—*how you feel.* The
only comparisons you need ever make to achieve peak performances are inner comparisons. You compare how you feel
when acting from strengths to how you feel when acting from
weaknesses.

What we want you to do is start reaching peak performances in many areas of your life. By peak performance we
mean simply doing something better than you usually do, and
by better we mean so that you enjoy it more *and* achieve
more.

FACTORS THAT PRODUCE PEAK PERFORMING

Dr. Gayle Privette, associate professor of psychology at
the University of West Florida, questioned 120 men and
women to see if there were certain factors common to
peak performance in such widely different fields as
science, art, and sports.

She found three distinctive personality characteristics
that were present during peak performing:

Spontaneity. The peak performance is purposeful
but breaks both "inner restraints and outer limitations." The person feels a complete coming together
of their inner and outer selves.

Clear Focus. "The peak performance is marked by
full focus on one subject." This is what we call clarity;
a person performing at his best concentrates on every-

thing that is important to the activity and on nothing that is irrelevant.

Feelings of Strength and Vitality. This intense feeling awareness "grows from the mobilization of the whole being. . . . If the expression of the whole being is in words, the person is lucid and articulate; if it is in lifting an object, he is strong; in running, he is fast; his whole being is speaking, lifting or running."

For example, suppose you are sometimes very shy when meeting people. The best reason to change is that you believe you will feel better by being more outgoing and outspoken. If you are trying to be what you want to be, then you can tell from your own feelings what feels good and what doesn't.

Of course it's desirable and helpful to choose models— people you admire and would like to imitate. Pick out a person you know well who isn't shy and get him to tell you about his life. You might be surprised to find that he was not always the way he is now.

MIRROR, MIRROR ON THE WALL

There is a saying that "at twenty you have the face you were born with; at forty the face you have earned." Look in the mirror right now. Do you like the person you see? Imagine yourself five years from now. How will you look? Will you feel better or worse about yourself? Will you like yourself more? Imagine yourself ten years from now and twenty years from now. When you picture your future, don't just picture a change in your circumstances. Picture yourself becoming more and more fit so that you like what you see and you like how you feel.

CONCLUSIONS

Psychological fitness is a new psychology. Many older people lose psychological power as they age. It is an unnecessary loss and waste. We think that people should become wiser and more fit as they age. In fact we think it is a necessity.

Psychological fitness is about having a life which doesn't rely on scrapbooks and memories for high points. It is the psychology of adult change and growth. An overall peak performance means that your personality skills and your personality power increase year by year. It means your forms of expression become more varied, it means your activity takes on subtle nuances, it means your feelings have greater depth, it means your clarity is expansive, and it means your contact is broad and inclusive. We think that it is not only a necessity that you have psychological fitness but a right. It is your right to express, it is your right to feel, it is your right to be active, it is your right to be clear, it is your right to have friends. We think that it is your right to have a life that is all that it can be, a life that is satisfying and exciting.

Information about
Psychological Fitness Training

Psychological Fitness Training Programs are offered through the Center Foundation. The Foundation is a nonprofit educational, research, and service organization based in Los Angeles with affiliated Psychological Fitness Training Centers located in various parts of the United States and the world.

Two main types of Fitness Training Programs are offered through the Center Foundation: a one-week intensive program that covers all areas of psychological fitness, and a series of eleven one-day psychological fitness training programs that are offered at bimonthly intervals. Special versions of both of these programs are available to various professional groups including lawyers, teachers, physicians, and business executives. (The Center also offers special Psychological Fitness Training Programs for corporations, schools, and government groups.)

A third program is The Associate Program. It is designed for those people who cannot attend training sessions in person. The Associate Program consists of guided at-home fitness training with written and phone follow-ups from a fitness counselor.

For information about these programs write:

Administrative Secretary
The Center Foundation
7165 Sunset Blvd.
Los Angeles, California 90046

The programs and ideas of psychological fitness are derived from a specific therapy, Feeling Therapy, and a general orientation to psychotherapy and counseling called the Functional Approach. Feeling Therapy is an intensive, long-term, community-based psychotherapy which is offered only at the Center for Feeling Therapy in Los Angeles. The Functional Approach to Counseling and Psychotherapy combines features of Humanistic Psychotherapy, Analytic Psychotherapy, and Behavior Therapy into an integrated theory and method for feeling better and functioning better. The Training Center for Functional Psychotherapy and Counseling is located in Los Angeles, with branches in other major cities.

Although Psychological Fitness Training originally developed from a psychotherapeutic context, the direction of influence is now two-way. We believe that the ideas and methods of psychological fitness are so powerful and effective that they will eventually replace the medical model of psychological treatment. We also believe that the fitness emphasis in psychology, psychotherapy, and counseling is much more desirable and more widely effective than the traditional mental health and mental hygiene emphases.

We welcome the participation of other professionals in both Psychological Fitness Programs and the Functional Approach to Counseling and Psychotherapy. For more information write:

Programs Director
The Training Center for Functional
    Psychotherapy and Counseling
7165 Sunset Blvd.
Los Angeles, California 90046

Recommended Reading
Related to Psychological Fitness

Listed below are some recommended books that correspond to the different sections of *Psychological Fitness*. We have drawn upon a wide variety of sources because the concepts and methods of psychological fitness overlap many disciplines, including medicine, psychology, physical education, sports and games, anthropology, psychotherapy and counseling, community planning, and political science.

Foreword and Part 1

Allport, G. W. *Becoming*. New Haven: Yale University Press, 1955. (Dr. Allport's ideas provide a major theoretical base for humanistic psychology and psychotherapy and for practical approaches to personality change.)

Ardell, D. B. *High Level Wellness*. Emmaus, Pennsylvania: Rodale Press, 1977. (A very convincing argument is presented in this book that wellness is different from worseness and that every individual must take responsibility for his or her health.)

Bradburn, N. *The Structure of Psychological Well-Being*. Chicago:

Aldine Publishing Company, 1969. (This is an important book of research and theory. Dr. Bradburn demonstrates that self-reports of happiness have considerable validity when measured against outside standards. He discovered that variations in positive and negative effect are independent of one another and that the two dimensions of well-being are correlated with different events and attitudes. Dr. Bradburn argues that mental health can best be promoted and sought by focusing on the concept of psychological well-being.)

Evans, R. *Carl Rogers: The Man and His Ideas.* New York: Dutton, 1975. (A dialogue in which Dr. Rogers reviews many of the ideas he developed that are now at the core of humanistic psychotherapy.)

Farb, P. *Humankind.* Boston: Houghton Mifflin, 1978. (A fact-filled survey of the social sciences.)

Fixx, J. *The Complete Book of Running.* New York: Random House, 1977. (A good general book on training, pushing limits, maximum performances, changing the way you live, and facts on physical fitness in America.)

Jahoda, M. *Current Concepts of Positive Mental Health.* New York: Basic Books, Inc., 1958. (Dr. Marie Jahoda says that the characteristics that make for good mental health are: self-identity, being in touch with feelings, a sense of the future, and a fruitful investment in life.)

Knowles, J. H., ed. *Doing Better and Feeling Worse: Health in the United States.* New York: W. W. Norton, 1977. (A book that is filled with facts and suggestions about health in the U.S.)

Lifton, R. J. *Boundaries: Psychological Man in Revolution.* New York: Touchstone, 1967. (Essays about the reality and unreality of psychological boundaries.)

Maslow, A. H. *The Farther Reaches of Human Nature.* New York: The Viking Press, 1971. (This book brings together many of Maslow's ideas about humanistic biology, self-actualizing, and peak experiences.)

Montagu, A. *Touching.* New York: Harper & Row, 1971. (A very good discussion about the need for touching throughout life.)

Morehouse, L. E., and L. Gross. *Maximum Performance.* New York: Simon & Schuster, 1977. (Another interesting book by the authors of *Total Fitness.*)

Morehouse, L. E., and L. Gross. *Total Fitness.* New York: Pocket Books, 1976. (This book represents the theory and practice of heart-rated exercise, pulse tests, and the use of guided overloads in exercising.)

Pelletier, K. R. *Mind as Healer, or Mind as Slayer.* New York: Delta, 1977. (General information about stress, psychosomatic ailments, and "the holistic approach to preventing stress disorders.")

Scarf, M. *Body, Mind, Behavior.* New York: Laurel, 1976. (A good popular survey of modern perspectives in psychology.)

Selye, H. *Stress without Distress.* New York: Signet, 1975. (Dr. Selye is the scientist who developed the idea of the general adaptation syndrome, the nonspecific response of the body to stress. He discusses in this book how to effectively *use* stress.)

Valiant, G. *Adaptation to Life.* Boston: Little, Brown & Company, 1977. (A fascinating research report about the psychological characteristics that make for a more successful adaptation to life throughout the human life cycle.)

Weiner, H. *Psychobiology and Human Disease.* New York: Elsevier, 1977. (A very important survey of psychosomatic medicine.)

Wooden, J. *They Call Me Coach.* New York: Bantam, 1973. (In his book Wooden describes the different ways he would respond to different players to enhance the player's strengths and help him change his weaknesses. He comments, "There is a very fine line between the champion and the runner-up" that is crossed only by equal attention to physical and psychological fitness.)

Zunin, L., and N. Zunin. *Contact: The First Four Minutes.* New York: Ballantine, 1972. (An easy-to-read book about the importance of touching and talking in every aspect of life.)

Part 2

Bannister, R. *The Four-Minute Mile.* London: Putnam & Company, 1955. (Before Bannister broke the four-minute barrier, the record of 4:01.4 had held for nine years; after Bannister's run on May 6, 1954, and up to July 1, 1961, the barrier was broken sixty-seven times by twenty-six runners from fourteen countries. Bannister believes the four-minute barrier was as much a psychological as a physical barrier—"a challenge to the human spirit.")

Coates, T. J., and C. E. Thoreson. *How to Sleep Better.* Englewood Cliffs, N.J.: Prentice-Hall, 1977. (The authors present a "drug-free program for overcoming insomnia"—as many as six out of ten people in the U.S. suffer from insomnia.)

Corriere, R., and J. Hart. *The Dream Makers.* New York: Funk &

Wagnalls, 1977; Bantam, 1978. (We present a practical program for using dreams to change personality dynamics.)

Jampol, H. *The Weekend Athlete's Way to a Pain-Free Monday.* New York: Hawthorn Books, 1973. (A simple and effective program of stretch exercises for physical fitness.)

Kolton, J. F. *Eat and Run: Your 1978 Diet, Exercise and Engagement Calendar.* New York: Holt, Rinehart & Winston, 1977. (Keep track of what you do, what you eat, and what you play.)

Leonard, G. *The Ultimate Athlete.* New York: Avon, 1977. (The author presents the humanistic approach to games, play, and exercise, using sports to develop the personality.)

Murphy, M. *Golf in the Kingdom.* New York: The Viking Press, 1972. (Michael Murphy is a co-founder of the Esalen Institute, which has long been a center for explorations of fitness and health. In this book he explains the inner game of golf as a regimen for stretching your personality.)

Progoff, I. *At a Journal Workshop.* New York: Dialogue House, 1975. (A guidebook to the use of a psychological journal for personal growth.)

Rainer, T. *The New Diary.* Los Angeles: J. P. Tarcher, 1978. (How to use a diary to explore personality changes.)

Sizer, N. F., and T. R. Sizer. *Five Lectures on Moral Education.* Cambridge, Mass.: Harvard University Press, 1970. (Lectures by James Gustafson, Richard Peters, Lawrence Kohlberg, Bruno Bettelheim, and Kenneth Keniston on the need for moral education.)

Part 3

Gordon, S. *Lonely in America.* New York: Simon & Schuster, 1976. (The author talks about loneliness as a human emotion that one should not be ashamed of but should talk about and take steps to change.)

Henry, J. P., and P. M. Stephens. *Stress, Health and the Social Environment.* New York: Springer-Verlag New York, 1977. (This is a very important book on the sociobiologic approach to medicine.)

Lewis, J., et al. *No Single Tread: Psychological Health in Family Systems.* New York: Brunner/Mazel, 1976. (This book reports on a research investigation of family psychological health—it is one of the few studies of health and positive functioning.)

Lynch, J. J. *The Broken Heart.* New York: Basic Books, 1977. (This is a valuable book about the serious medical consequences of loneliness.)

Schachter, S. *Emotion, Obesity and Crime.* New York: Academic Press, 1971. (This book includes experiments which demonstrate the social set and cognitive meanings that contribute to obesity.)

Sutherland, E. A., and Z. Amit. *Phobia Free.* New York: Stein & Day, 1977. (The authors present a practical self-help program, based on behavior therapy, for working with phobias.)

Zimbardo, P. G. *Shyness.* Reading, Mass.: Addison-Wesley, 1977. (A good guide to understanding shyness and what to do about it.)

Afterword and Appendices

Binder, V., A. Binder, and B. Rimland, eds. *Modern Therapies.* Englewood Cliffs, N.J.: Prentice-Hall, 1976. (This book contains chapters about many contemporary therapies that have contributed to a fitness approach, including Feeling Therapy, Rational-Emotive Therapy, Gestalt Therapy, Transactional Analysis, Reality Therapy, and Behavior Modification.)

Burrow, T. *A Search for Man's Sanity.* New York: Oxford University Press, 1958. (Trigant Burrow, a contemporary of Freud and Jung, is one of the forgotten pioneers of functional psychotherapy and the psychological fitness approach. He was so far ahead of his times that his writings still sound radical.)

Erikson, E. H., ed. *Adulthood.* New York: W. W. Norton, 1978. (The book contains essays by scholars from many disciplines about the meaning of adulthood in different cultures.)

Frank, J. D. *Persuasion and Healing: A Comparative Study of Psychotherapy.* New York: Schocken, 1974. (A modern classic about the many forms and modes of healing in different societies.)

Hart, J., R. Corriere, and J. Binder. *Going Sane: An Introduction to Feeling Therapy.* New York: Dell/Delta, 1975. (This book describes the theory, practice, and structure of Feeling Therapy, from which many of the basic ideas and methods of the psychological fitness program are developed.)

Hart, J., et al. *The Functional Approach to Dreams.* New York: Harcourt Brace Jovanovich, not yet published. (This forthcoming book presents the functional approach to dreams and psychotherapy and relates the functional method of working with dreams and waking to other methods.)

James, W. *Pragmatism and Other Essays.* New York: Pocket Books, 1963. (Pragmatism and functional psychology as developed by William James, John Dewey, and others are the historical antecedents for functional psychotherapy and the psychological fitness approach.)

London, P. *The Modes and Morals of Psychotherapy.* New York: Holt, Rinehart & Winston, 1964. (This book represents an early attempt to bring together "insight" and "action" therapies.)

Rappaport, J. *Community Psychology.* New York: Holt, Rinehart & Winston, 1977. (This is a textbook about the modern field of community psychology.)

Schumacher, E. F. *A Guide for the Perplexed.* New York: Harper & Row, 1977. (A plea for the development of the inner life: "man's happiness is to move higher, to develop his highest faculties.")

Stevenson, J. *Issues and Crises in Middlescence.* New York: Appleton-Century-Crofts, 1977. (The author discusses the stages of growth in middle age and the importance of continued growth and activity throughout life.)

Index